## Secrets of the Face:
## Your Character and Future Revealed
*Jocelyne Cooke*

The ancient Chinese recognized that the character and future of a person could be read in the features of his or her face. They were very aware that the location of the ears, the size of the earlobes, or the shape of the chin were very indicative of the person's nature.
This book presents a detailed description of our facial features, according to size, shape, color, and location, and explains how they mold our characters and influence our future. By means of the ancient Chinese art of face-reading, our quality of life can be improved.

Jocelyne Cooke lives in Sydney. In the early 1980s, she visited the Philippines, Hong Kong, China, and Japan, and met up with people who were interested in various mystical methods of character analysis and predicting the future. She was fascinated by the Chinese method of "reading" the body and the face, and she spent several years in the Far East perfecting the arts. She then went to Los Angeles, and, after a three-year stay, returned to Australia, where she practices these arts.
Jocelyne Cooke is also the author of "Secrets of the Body: Your Character and Future Revealed."

# ASTROLOG COMPLETE GUIDES SERIES

The Complete Guide to Coffee Grounds and Tea Leaf Reading
*Sara Zed*

The Complete Guide to Palmistry
*Batia Shorek*

The Complete Guide to Tarot Reading
*Hali Morag*

Crystals - Types, Use and Meaning
*Connie Islin*

The Dictionary of Dreams
*Eili Goldberg*

Meditation: The Journey to Your Inner World
*Eidan Or*

Playing Cards: Predicting Your Future
*Hali Morag*

Day-by-Day Numerology
*Lia Robin*

Using Astrology To Choose Your Partner
*Amanda Starr*

The I Ching
*Nizan Weisman*

Pendulums
*Jared O'Keefe*

Channeling
*Roxanne McGuire*

What Moles Tell You About Yourself
*Pietro Santini*

Secrets of the Body: Your Character and Future Revealed
*Jocelyne Cooke*

Secrets of the Face: Your Character and Future Revealed
*Jocelyne Cooke*

Astrology
*Amanda Starr*

Day-by-Day Wicca
*Tabatha Jennings*

# Secrets of the
# FACE

Your Character and Future Revealed

## Jocelyne Cooke
with
## Sarah Letton

Astrolog Publishing House

Astrolog Publishing House
P. O. Box 1123, Hod Hasharon 45111, Israel
Tel: 972-9-7412044
Fax: 972-9-7442714
E-Mail: info@astrolog.co.il
Astrolog Web Site: www.astrolog.co.il

© 2000 Jocelyne Cooke

ISBN 965-494-106-6

All rights reserved. No part of this publication may be reproduced, stored in a retrieval system, or transmitted in any form or by any means, electronic, mechanical, photocopying, recording or otherwise, without the prior permission of the publisher.

Published by Astrolog Publishing House 2000

Printed in Israel
10 9 8 7 6 5 4 3 2 1

# CONTENTS

| | |
|---|---|
| Introduction | 6 |
| Yin and Yang | 11 |
| The Shape of the Face | 15 |
| The Three Milestones of Life | 24 |
| The Twelve Facial Mansions | 27 |
| The Profile of the Forehead | 42 |
| The Profile of the Ears | 49 |
| The Profile of the Eyes | 56 |
|     The Eyebrows | 67 |
| The Profile of the Nose | 77 |
|     The Nostrils | 84 |
|     The Philtrum | 86 |
| The Profile of the Cheekbones | 88 |
| The Profile of the Mouth | 92 |
|     The Teeth | 103 |
| The Profile of the Chin | 105 |
|     The Jawline | 108 |

# INTRODUCTION

The history of Chinese Face Reading can be traced back to just over two thousand years ago. Records of this art date from the sixth century BC. The Chinese, however, are not the only people to believe in the mysterious power of this art. The ancient Greeks also used the face to elicit information about a person's character and true self. There is one difference between Chinese Face Reading and the ancient Greeks' Physiognomy: whereas the Chinese art concentrates purely on the face, Physiognomy is concerned with the whole body. However, this does not mean that the ancient Greeks did not attribute considerable importance to the facial structure. Incidentally, the Greeks tended to use more planetary associations than the Chinese when describing the face.

In ancient China, there were many different schools of thought. These varied sects each taught, lived by, and explored different philosophies. As the years passed, the number of existing schools gradually decreased. Unfortunately, as they disappeared, so did a great deal of their knowledge, teachings, theories and practices. Not all of this information was lost to us, however, and over recent years the western world as whole has become far more receptive to and interested in the secrets of this eastern country.

There are various styles of Chinese Face Reading that have managed to survive the ages and that are still in practice today. The information in this book derives from one of the ancient schools of thoughts.

The Chinese divided the face in to two categories: the Five

## Secrets of the FACE

Main Traits and the Seven Defining Traits. The Five Main Traits are the ears, eyes, eyebrows, nose, and mouth. The Main Traits are very important as they are linked to success and achievement in life. By examining these traits, you can learn not only about your possibilities and potential with regard to your career ambitions, but also with regard to your home and love lives. The Seven Defining Traits are the areas under your eyes, your forehead, cheekbones, chin, jaw-line, laugh lines, and philtrum (the groove running from under your nose to your upper lip). Whereas the Five Main Traits represent your potential (that you can choose to use to your advantage or not), the Defining Traits tell you about the influences, situations and opportunities that will come into your life whether you want them to or not; the people, events, coincidences and general occurrences that constitute the hand that Fate has decided to deal you.

There are two levels of examination that you must try and learn to combine in order to perform a full and accurate face reading. First of all, get a general overview of the face that you are reading. Without letting any personal bias affect your view, try to understand the kind of feeling the face gives you about the person. Once you have a sense of the face, it makes it far easier to perform a significant reading. Next, you need to move on to examine the individual features. This can be quite a lengthy process, but as you become more familiar with the art of Chinese Face Reading, you will be able to provide faster readings. With enough practice, you won't even need to refer to this book at all!

Finally, once you have completed the individual trait readings, try to put all of your information together to provide a broad interpretation. This is the tricky bit. It can be frustrating at first, when you're not quite able to link all of the meanings together. But as you learn, everything will become clearer to you, and the final stage – the conclusion of the reading – will become fuller and richer as you progress.

Some of the analyses may not say what you were hoping to hear. Perhaps one trait on your face points to a negative or unpleasant aspect of your character or life. Don't be alarmed. In Chinese Face Reading, even negativity is ultimately a positive thing. For example, your eyes may signify that you are an impulsive person who leaves much to chance. Your analysis may say that this could have a negative impact on your personal and professional life. Rather than waiting in dread for everything to fall apart around you, the wisest course of action (and what the analysis is actually implying) is to learn to tone down your impulsiveness and control it. Some situations will actually benefit from these qualities, but other scenarios are damaged by such behavior. Learn to take the bad with the good, and realize that knowledge truly is power. You have the power to change things for the better once you know and understand how you are blocking your future good by wasting time on negative energies and unsuitable behavior.

Even if one or two of your traits appear to be negative or have an interpretation that you find hard to accept, you must remember that the surrounding traits have a direct connection, and that their positivity will weaken the surrounding negativity (and vice versa!).

Before you begin reading your face, it would be

worthwhile getting yourself a little mirror; being able to look at your face will not only allow you to examine it as you go along, but will make it a little easier to actually locate certain reference points.

The book itself has been set out in an easy-to-follow formula, with the analyses flowing easily from one to the next. You will also find a trait profile at the beginning of each section (where it's relevant). This should help you to get a relatively easy, yet nicely detailed analysis of your own or someone else's face. Please take note of the information (such as moles, lines, etc.) at the end of some of the sections. You may also find it helpful to have some paper and a pen at hand to jot down any particularly interesting analysis. If you make notes as you go along, it is far easier to compare all of the analyses of individual traits, and weave them into a full, complete work.

The rationale behind Chinese Face Reading is not as obscure and unfounded as you may at first believe. Today our level of scientific knowledge and technology is incredible. Available scientific information about the face even allows us to reconstruct a face based on the remains of a skull two or three thousand years old. Over the years, many scientific and sociological studies have been conducted on the possible links between facial structures and personality and character type. It has been found that there are certain sorts of facial structure that *are* linked to specific types of social (and anti-social) behavior and interaction. Some scientists have claimed that they have identified certain facial characteristics from which they can predict levels of achievement, intelligence, life potential – and even a predilection for certain occupational fields. Essentially, it is now the opinion of some scientists that our genes not only shape us physically, but also have a direct influence on our future lives.

There are a lot of people in the world who would ridicule Chinese Face Reading, or any other such art. Tarot cards, runes, and palmistry, for example, are all open to the cynicism and scorn of many people. The idea that various kinds of divination and spirituality cannot be *disproved* is not enough to make those people believe.

The simple fact remains that, true or false, real or not, cynic or believer, it is good and enriching to learn about and experience as much in life as possible.

# YIN AND YANG

I'm sure that you have heard of Yin and Yang. This union, which is the epitome of harmony and balance, is most usually represented and recognized in the western world as a black and white circle made up of two tadpole-shaped halves that curl into each other. The black half has a small white dot – like an eye – and the white half has a black dot. This sharing of each other's color represents the balance, compromise and complete acceptance of the two halves. The Yin is completed by a little of the Yang influence, and likewise, the Yang finds peace through absorbing some Yin energy.

The Chinese have very strong roots in the philosophy of natural energies, and strive to achieve their correct balance and combination. Yin and Yang are a partnership that the Chinese hold in high esteem – the alliance forming the ideal relationship in terms of balance. According this particular ancient art, the face is made up of both Yin and Yang energies.

**RIGHT**  **LEFT**
**YIN**  **YANG**

Your face as a whole is Yang. Your forehead, cheekbones, nose, jaw-line and chin are all Yang. To remember these traits, all you have to do is associate Yang with all of the more prominent traits of your face – those made of bone or cartilage. Yang represents the universe's masculine energies, daytime, creativity and also action. Yang also represents your workplace – even if your work is in the home. With regard to your home, don't forget that Yang is directly connected with the structure (the bricks and mortar). So, for example, if your face as a whole is Yang-dominant, then you are probably very ambitious and industrious, as well as able to build (metaphorically or literally) successfully. Your career is likely to be full of great achievements, and you will play a very active role in attaining your success. You are able to achieve financial security through your work. As Yang dominance is also valid for the building in which you will live, it's probable that you will be able to buy a good, large and secure home.

When your face is divided vertically into two halves, Yang occupies the left side. If you are Yang-dominant according to this definition, then the above still applies to you. Some of your character traits mean that you are destined for success. You are very strong, not only in terms of emotional and mental energies, but also regarding your will, which makes you extremely determined and single-minded. Combine this with your ambition, and the sky is the limit! You are basically a very straight and truthful person, and you can be very patient with people and situations. However, sometimes you upset or offend people unintentionally simply because you tend to speak the truth very bluntly. It's not that you mean to offend anyone – it's just that you can be harsh and even stubborn when trying to get a point across; don't forget that

Yang is also associated with aggression. If you could muster a little more diplomacy, you could probably go places a lot faster – and the journey there would be a lot smoother, too!

The right side of your face is the half that belongs to Yin. Yin relates to all of the softer, fleshier parts of your face – for example, the end of your nose, your lips, the flesh on your cheeks, your eyebrows, eyelashes, etc. As you can expect, Yin is everything that Yang isn't. Yin represents feminine cosmic energies, pleasure, the night, the spiritual and emotional, and the maternal. You're Yin-dominant if the bone structure of your face (the Yang features) is covered nicely with soft, firm flesh. Your nose, chin and jaw-line are not sharp at all. This kind of face usually looks warm, friendly and kind. Although you have the ability to do very well in life, unfortunately you may actually be hindering instead of helping yourself. People who are Yin-dominant are liable to be passive; they let others guide or even lead them, instead of getting up and doing their own thing. It's this passive nature that could be holding you back. If you never set challenges for yourself, or believe that you can achieve high goals, you will never make any major breakthroughs in your life. It would be a great shame if such a good and talented person were never to reach his or her full potential!

Yin is related not to the structure of your home, but to the contents – all of your worldly possessions! As a person with Yin dominance, its is likely that your home is a little palace! It is probably well decorated and really comfortable, with luxurious little touches. If your financial situation is preventing you from having your dream home, you can rest assured that when the time is right, you will get what you want!

## Secrets of the FACE

The ideal face is balanced, its two halves being equal. In everyday life, though, there are very, very few symmetrically balanced faces. The Chinese simply believe that a balance between Yin and Yang in a person's face shows that the individual is incredibly balanced in every way – mentally and physically, emotionally and rationally, materially and spiritually, and, of course, there is a fine-tuned balance between their inner masculine and feminine energies.

# THE SHAPE OF THE FACE

The shape of your face reveals more about you than you may realize. We guess age by looking at the face, and we can tell how someone is feeling by their facial expressions. In Chinese Face Reading, you can also learn how to analyze a person's true character and personality by studying the shape of their face. Once you have familiarized yourself with the following types of face and what their meaning is, you will find that you can see into a person's soul the very moment you are introduced.

According to this ancient art, there are five basic types of face. They are referred to as *elemental types*. These types are directly linked to the planetary elements that include *Fire*, *Water*, *Wood*, *Earth* and *Gold* (also known as *Metal*).

Although the primary concern is the shape of the face, use the complexion to add detail to your analysis. As you read the following analyses, you will see that each type is given its own Vital Energy, Fate and Field. Remember to take note of those that apply to you – they are the keys to your future success and happiness!

**ROUND** – rounded forehead and chin, broadest at the cheeks.

WATER TYPE
VITAL ENERGY – ADAPTABILITY
FATE – RICHES
FIELD – BUSINESS AND FINANCE
PLANET – MERCURY

You are extremely amenable, which enables you to be easily accepted by all the different types of people. Your adaptable nature is complemented by your charm and diplomacy – a perfect combination for the financial and business worlds of "wheeling and dealing."

It is not impossible, however, for you to use your positive qualities for negative purposes – your own gain. A desire for a quick buck may cause an opportunistic character to develop, and it could be difficult for others to distinguish between the real you and the facade.

**SQUARE** – square jaw and hairline, face of equal width and length.

EARTH TYPE
VITAL ENERGY – TRANQUILLITY
FATE – SECURITY
FIELD – INDUSTRY
PLANET – SATURN

You possess a core of determination, will power and patience. You are thoughtful and trustworthy; a promise is a promise. You seek a stable home and family life, and will move heaven and earth to achieve this. The above qualities also make you a formidable force in the business world, and you are able to build huge empires.

While will power enables you to remain true to your strong principles, don't be tempted to take it to an unreasonable limit. Obstinate to the last, you are inclined to cut your nose off to spite your face, and may become set in your ways. Take care not to develop an aggressive streak.

## Secrets of the FACE

**RECTANGULAR** – face is longer than it is wide, uniform width.

GOLD TYPE
VITAL ENERGY – GRACE
FATE – PRESTIGE
FIELD – MANAGEMENT
PLANET – VENUS

You have wonderful social skills, a natural grace, and elegance. These attributes, in conjunction with good manners, indicate that you are destined to reach the pinnacle of your chosen field. You will be well respected and esteemed by others. For you, wealth and riches seem to fall from the sky – but be warned: Your seemingly easy path through life may lead you to become conceited and lazy. If everything in life is given to you on a silver platter, why work for anything?

**PEAR-SHAPED** – narrow at the forehead and temples, broadening at the jaw-line.

FIRE TYPE
VITAL ENERGY – ACTION
FATE – ADVENTURE
FIELD – ENTERTAINER
PLANET – MARS

You are an extrovert with natural charisma, which means you are never short of friends. You like people and have a palpable warmth. All of this means that you are a born performer, and the ideal occupation for you is one where you can utilize this to the full. The well of energy you possess means that you are always on the go.

If this vigor is allowed to get out of control, though, it can manifest itself in nervous energy; you have a tendency to flit from one thing to another or from one person or project to the next, without ever giving your full attention to any of them. Your connection with Mars also implies that you have a quick temper that you should learn to curb.

**TRIANGULAR** – broad forehead, face narrowing to a pointed chin (inverted triangle).

WOOD TYPE
VITAL ENERGY – ASCENDING
FATE – INTELLECT
FIELD – ACADEME
PLANET – JUPITER

You are idealistic, honest, and sincere. Constantly searching for answers to eternal esoteric questions, you are the most intellectual of all the types. Your perceptive and intuitive exploration of the spiritual plane means that you notice the small nuances in life that so many others miss. An inquiring and artistic mind guides you toward education – for your own edification, or teaching others. Your riches lie in knowledge rather than in wealth.

Your tendency to float far from the terrestrial realm may (fairly or unfairly) expose you to the ridicule of others. Reach for the stars, but see that you keep one foot on the ground!

## COMBINATIONS OF SHAPES

While some faces are easy to define in terms of their shape, others may be more complicated. You may find it hard to decide on the shape of your face because it is not simply one particular type, but is, in fact, a combination of two types. To make things easier, check to see where the broadest part of your face is, and then decide which type best describes your facial shape.

**DIAMOND** – prominent features, narrow chin and forehead, widest at cheekbones.

WOOD-FIRE TYPE
VITAL ENERGY – CHANNELED ENERGY
FATE – TRIUMPH
FIELD – INNOVATION
PLANETS – MARS AND JUPITER
(See also triangle and pear-shape analyses.)

You are intelligent and have a healthy sense of competition (not just in material things). You also are fortunate to have a natural talent of some kind; be sure to discover and cultivate it for your success.

## Secrets of the FACE

**OVAL** – high forehead, small chin, overall shape of an elongated circle.

WOOD – GOLD TYPE
VITAL ENERGY – EMOTIONS
FATE – ESTHETIC
FIELD – ACTING, HAUTE COUTURE
PLANETS – VENUS AND JUPITER
(See also triangular and oblong analyses.)

This is the face of stereotypical ideal feminine beauty and male good looks. Many famous models, actors and actresses – past and present – belong to this type. You have innate style and elegance. Your path in life may have been smooth and easy to follow during your younger years, but a lack of will power and inner mental strength in your adult years may mean that it has become a little rocky. You would be wise to develop these qualities in preparation for the years ahead.

**HEART-SHAPED** – small pointed chin, rounded jaw, widest at the forehead with a "widow's peak."

WOOD-WATER TYPE
VITAL ENERGY – CONTROL
FATE – CONGENIALITY
FIELD – CREATIVITY
PLANETS – JUPITER AND MERCURY
(See also round and triangular analyses.)

You have good social skills, meaning that you mix easily with people – individuals and groups alike – who are drawn to you by your positive attitude. You have skills, but if you are not careful, they will fail to come to fruition. Your own natural talents are in danger of remaining underdeveloped due to a possible dependency on controlling and manipulating other people for your own ends. Remember, ultimate success and happiness can only be achieved through true and honest efforts.

# THE THREE MILESTONES OF LIFE

There are three "milestones," each representing a different period of your life. The First Milestone covers your life from the age of 15 up to the age of 30. This milestone starts at your hairline, going down to your eyebrows. The Second Milestone represents your life between the ages of 31 and 50. It starts at your eyebrows and goes down your face to the base of your nose. The Third Milestone contains information about your life from the age of 50 onward. It starts at your nose and finishes at the tip of your chin. Pay particular attention to the milestone that applies to your current age. After all, what you do today will effect what you do tomorrow.

If all three milestones are the same size and your face divides into equal thirds, you should be grateful! Perfectly balanced milestones show that you are a person with a character and life of equilibrium. Your rounded personality is developed and balanced; a steady and fortunate upbringing has prepared you for achievement in early adulthood, a pleasant middle age, and a happy old age leading to a successful life conclusion.

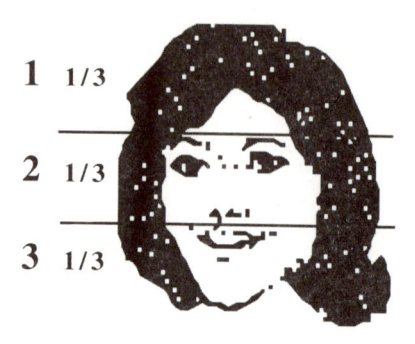

It's more likely though, that you will notice that your milestones are not all the same size. If one of your milestones is larger than the others, it is the dominant milestone. If you have a noticeably smaller milestone than the others, it is a stunted milestone. Don't worry if this sounds a bit confusing at this point. As you read the following analyses, everything should become clearer!

**THE FIRST MILESTONE**

The First Milestone starts at your hairline and goes down to your eyebrows. It is concerned with your life from the age of 15 to 30 years. If your First Milestone is dominant, it denotes a busy and successful start in life. You probably have a colorful history, rich with many experiences (good or bad). What you have learned during this stage of your life has aided your personal development, and you have a firm footing that enables you to embark upon life confidently.

If your First Milestone is stunted, it shows that you probably didn't have a particularly fortuitous start in life. It's likely that you weren't given many opportunities, and that your parents did not give you the kind of love, support and encouragement that you felt you needed. But through some sort of hardship, you have developed strength of character, which stands you in good stead for the future. Just remember that you have the experience and the abilities to take quantum leaps in your life – but to do this successfully, you must be able to let go of your past and any negativity connected to it. Learn to let go of anything that could be holding you back.

## THE SECOND MILESTONE

The Second Milestone starts at your eyebrows and ends at the base of your nose. It covers your life between the ages of 31 and 50. If your Second Milestone predominates, you can expect to reach the pinnacle of success during this middle section of your life. You will be fulfilled and financially secure, with a happy home and personal life, too.

Should your Second Milestone be noticeably stunted, you may not settle down in a career, and basically you'll be a "late developer," whose success comes at a later stage. By the time you enter your third stage of life, you will probably look back on this time with a sense of pride at the challenges and vicissitudes that you have managed to overcome.

## THE THIRD MILESTONE

This final milestone begins at the base of your nose and covers the lower third of your face to the end of your chin. This milestone tells you about your life from the age of 50 and onwards. A dominant Third Milestone means that during this part of your life, you will enjoy the fruits of your labor! The hard work you put into the earlier stages of your life has paid off, and you will provide for yourself with ease. You can relax and revel in the company of those you love most.

A stunted Third Milestone indicates troubles in later life as a result of financial worries, ill health, or the absence of loved ones to take care of you. So, in order to make the most of this time and to find peace of mind, you must ensure that you are in peak physical condition and that you are financially secure. Hopefully, though, you will have laid a firm financial foundation during the previous stages. Experience will have expanded your horizons, and life will be good to you – so long as you approach it in the right way.

# THE TWELVE FACIAL MANSIONS

The mansions are points on your face that can help guide you through your undertakings in life. By locating and examining them, you can discover where you need to direct and focus your energies, thus helping yourself to reach your goals and find happiness and success. Once familiar with the mansions, you can also use your knowledge to find out some little secrets of those around you!

**The Mansion of Life:** Life can be tough. Use this mansion to learn how to make your life a little easier.

**The Mansions of Parents:** Whether good or bad, we all inherit something from our parents. Use what they gave you to your advantage.

**The Mansions of Brothers, Sisters, and Friends:** Find out you everything you need to know about your friends, brothers, and sisters.

**The Mansion of Success:** We can all get what we want. Find out how to unlock your potential and reach for the stars.

**The Mansions of Joy and Luck:** An educated guess is far better than a blind bet. Maximize your rewards by minimizing the risks.

**The Mansion of Health:** Your health is everything. Make sure you have a balance between body and mind.

**The Mansions of Moving:** Be sure that the time is right to make that special physical or mental move.

**The Mansions of Marriage:** We all want to find that special someone to share our life with. Eternal love could be staring you in the face.

**The Mansions of Children:** Creating a new life is a privilege. Do you have the eyes of parenthood?

**The Mansions of the Home:** Your home is your castle. Keep it in order so you can go forth into the world with confidence.

**The Mansions of Assets:** Protect your precious possessions – and your pocket.

**The Mansion of Riches:** You work hard for your money. Discover the secret of accumulating profit.

As you may have noticed, some of the mansions are plural; for example, the Mansions of the Home and the Mansions of Children, as opposed to the singular Mansion of Life. The reason behind this is simple. The plural mansions have not just one point of reference but two – one on the left side of the face, the other on the corresponding right side.

The mansion on the left symbolizes Yang (which is active). The mansion on the right represents Yin (which is passive). Refer back to the section on Yin and Yang, if necessary, as it will clarify the meanings and differences between the two.

Because of this duality, the twelve titled mansions actually constitute twenty separate points that you should examine regularly.

### The Mansion of Life

Your Mansion of Life lies between your eyebrows. In some cultures, this space is believed to contain the so-called "Third Eye." This potent third eye possesses magical and mysterious gifts: intuition and insight. We are all born with these two special things. Who can deny ever having a "gut feeling"? Without them, the soul withers and dies. We need to listen to these inner voices and feelings to help us smooth the path to success and happiness.

Before you make any decisions or changes that could have far-reaching repercussions in your life, you would be wise to consult with this mansion. Maybe you want to know whether you should go for that new job you saw advertised yesterday, or ask your boss for a promotion. The Mansion of Life cannot give you a simple "yes" or "no" in answer to your query, but it can show you whether you have the inner strength and vitality needed to properly pursue and successfully accomplish your coveted aim.

If your Mansion of Life has a healthy lilac glow, then go for it! Your energy is high and everything is in place for you to take your first step forward with confidence and clarity. On the other hand, if the mansion is too pale or too dark, this is not the most opportune moment to make your move. Be patient; wait until you have enough strength to get what you want.

## The Mansions of Parents

Imagine that you have two vertical lines running up from the middle of your eyebrows to your hairline. The Mansions of Parents are situated in the middle of these lines, halfway down your forehead. The right mansion is connected to your mother and her side of the family, the left signifies your father and his relatives.

Confusion could arise here if you are adopted. Should you relate these points to your biological (and possibly unknown) parents? Or do you rely on the mansions being influenced by your adoptive parents? Ultimately the choice is yours. Before you decide, though, you should remember that the genetic material passed on to you by your biological parents is not necessarily the most important thing. The most precious gift we get from our parents is their love and attention. It is the act of raising a child on a day-to-day basis that makes someone a parent. Ask the couple who have adopted a child if their love and parental instincts are any less because they didn't create the child they call their own. Their answer will surely be a resounding "no." Another fact to consider is that this mansion deals with what has shaped your personality, not your body. The people who brought you up have done this through instilling the values and beliefs that they themselves hold dear into you.

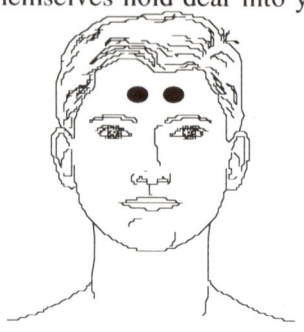

Consult these mansions if there is any kind of problem within your family structure. Did you forget your mother's birthday and have a row? If the mansion is pink and healthy, now would be a good time to take those flowers and apologize to her. Did you unintentionally insult your father when discussing politics last week? A pale mansion means that maybe you should give it another few days before you call him to bury the hatchet. You can also use these mansions as a warning system. If either mansion is pale or discolored, guard against upsetting either parent, and exercise diplomacy and tact. Remember to be sensitive to your family's needs. After all, blood is thicker than water.

### The Mansions of Brothers, Sisters, and Friends

These two mansions sit above the middle of the eyebrows. The mansion on the left relates to your friends, and the mansion on the right to your brothers and sisters (if you have any).

Let's start with the Mansions of Friends. This is Yang which, as we know, is active; you decide who your friends are; this is under your control. This mansion also covers social activities and business associates. If this area is pale, dark or otherwise discolored, you should not only exercise restraint and sensitivity in your dealings, but you should also be wary and not too quick to trust the words of those around you. This is not to say that you should be paranoid, though! If the color is pinkish and good, then you can rest assured that nothing unsavory is going on.

The Mansion of Brothers and Sisters is Yin, which is passive – meaning that you cannot choose your family. Again you are to consider the color of the mansions and act accordingly.

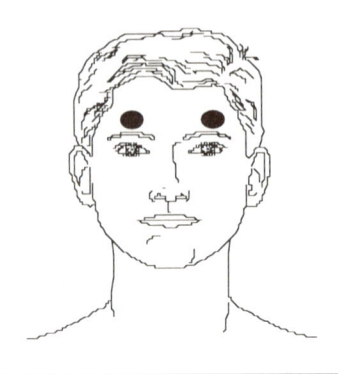

## The Mansion of Success

We all have something in life that we dream of achieving; whether in matters of education, business and finance, or affairs of the heart. The Mansion of Success stands proudly in the middle of your forehead just below the hairline. This mansion cannot tell you whether you will reach your objective – it simply indicates whether or not your current course of action is providing you with the best chance of success.

For example; if a lazy student is neglecting his or her studies, the chances of achieving good grades is low and this mansion would probably be pale or even gray. The student would be wise to turn down that party invitation and get down to those assignments that are piling up.

When the mansion is pink (and possibly glowing), you can be confident that you are applying the right amount of energy and thought to accomplishing your chosen goal. Stick with it and success will be yours. The human spirit is incredible, and almost anything is possible.

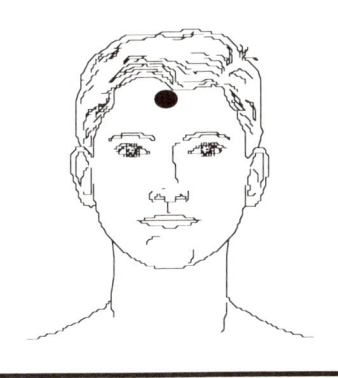

### The Mansions of Joy and Luck

These mansions sit comfortably on your temples. The mansion on the left is connected with happiness. It is Yang (active) and tells us of the happiness we bring ourselves. If this mansion is pale and has blemishes, then you need to rethink your choices and actions if you are to achieve the highest level of joy possible.

The mansion on the right tells us of our future luck. This mansion belongs to the passive Yin, meaning that the luck it speaks of is beyond our control. If this mansion is pale, don't despair; it doesn't mean that you have a black cloud hanging over you. Rather, it hints that you need to be more alert to and aware of what's going. Luck could actually be all around you; you just need to open your eyes, slow down and take notice.

Bear in mind that these two mansions can be especially significant if you are prone to gambling or placing the odd bet. Their color and condition can indicate when you are most likely to have good luck at the card table, races or roulette wheel.

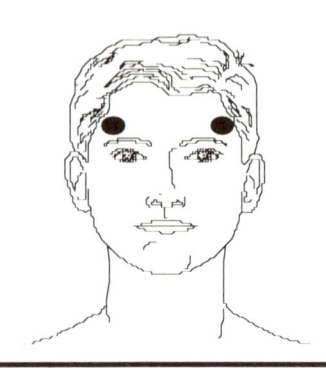

## The Mansion of Health

Your Mansion of Health is located in the "Third Eye" position, and warns you about potential dips in physical energy. It is important to remember that the only way that any of us can reach our full potential is to make sure that we are not neglecting our physical well-being. However, if you have any doubts about your health, it is paramount that you receive the attention and opinion of a fully qualified doctor.

You should examine this mansion if you are considering undertaking any change or project that will require you to be in good physical condition. You might be considering a change in diet, beginning a new form of exercise – or even starting a new job that will require a lot of physical energy. If the mansion is a healthy color and the skin is smooth and unblemished, then your energy levels are high, and you can go ahead with confidence. However, if this mansion is pale or dull, you would be best served by concentrating on fortifying your health before embarking on your plans.

Remember, you are far more likely to make a successful first step if you have the energy you need to take you to the end of your path.

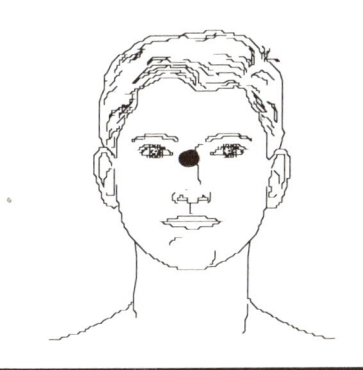

### The Mansions of Moving

There are two Mansions of Moving, each located on opposite corners of the forehead, just next to the hairline. As their name suggests, these mansions are connected with movement of some kind: possessions, property and, on a more metaphorical level, the mind. Each mansion corresponds with a different direction in movement.

The mansion on the left concerns things that are moving away from you. This could include letters and other forms of correspondence you send, journeys you undertake, or even something you're trying to sell. If this mansion is pale or discolored, be wary; you may not be getting the best price in that sale you're about to make. Also, guard against anything being lost or stolen.

If the mansion on the right has a nice pink hue, you can be sure that something is coming your way – a letter, a parcel, or even guests. Be ready to exchange contracts on your first home, or that country cottage you've been hoping to purchase. Is there a sale in your favorite department store? Now is a good time to get that outfit you've had your eye on. Remember that what you are about to receive need not necessarily be practical and tangible. You may find that you are to acquire some kind of knowledge, information or mental breakthrough that will help you in some way.

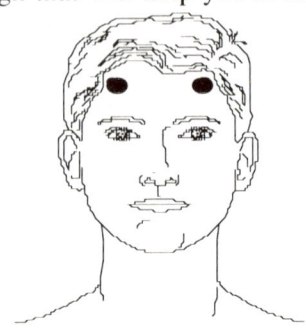

## The Mansions of Marriage

Your Mansions of Marriage nestle at the outer corner of your eyes, on top of your cheekbones. The mansion on the left is that of "Wives, Husbands and Children." Ideally this mansion should be smooth and firm. This indicates stability and happiness with your mate.

For matters of fidelity, examine the mansion on the right. You will probably want to use your knowledge of this mansion when looking for a potential partner, too! You should be concerned with the number of lines in this area. If this mansion has many lines, it implies sexual promiscuity in a person's younger years, which could possibly continue throughout adult life. Alternatively, these lines may signify the number of marriages or significant relationships that will take place during life's course. Either way, the more lined this mansion is, the less stability there will be unless you are careful in your choices.

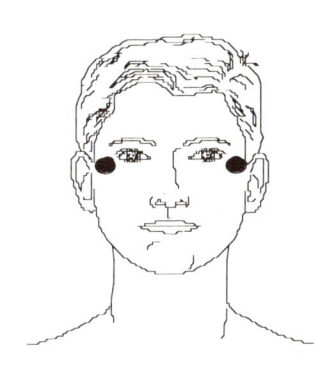

### The Mansions of Children

You'll find these two mansions under your eyes – right where those annoying bags appear when we're tired!

The mansion on the left is connected to your biological ability to have children, and the mansion on the right indicates the children that may come to you through remarriage (stepchildren), adoption or fostering. The differences between the two mansions are not particularly important, as both correspond to your levels of fertility and your sexual behavior – both of which have an effect on your child-bearing prospects.

A good level of fertility and a healthy sex life are shown when these mansions are well-fleshed (but not too puffy) and have the same color and tone as the rest of your face. On the other hand, should these mansions be swollen, hollow or discolored, you may be well advised to examine your lifestyle. These characteristics point to a low level of fertility possibly due to sexual excesses, which can cause health problems and affect your fertility. This is easy to rectify, however.

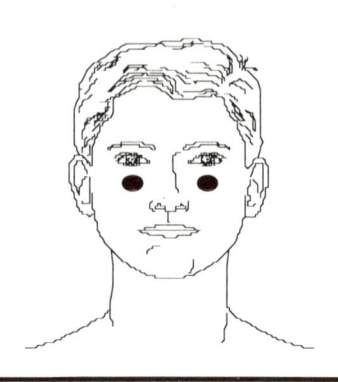

## The Mansions of the Home

These two mansions begin at the corners of your mouth and extend to your jawbone. In this context, "home" does not simply refer to your residence and its contents, but also to your body.

Let's look at your residence first. Running a household is no mean feat and there are many things to think about; building maintenance, repairs, possible damage, decoration, not to mention the things you do and have done around the house, and the small day-to-day things. The list is endless. If your mansions are lined and sagging, make sure that nothing is being neglected. Replace that section of old guttering, nail down that loose roof tile. Check your insurance; is that policy outdated? Before you make any alteration to your home or the way you run it, check the condition of these mansions.

Your physical well-being also falls under the shelter of these mansions. Again, should these areas be blemished, you would be wise to examine your lifestyle. Are you drinking or eating excessively? Now is a good time to stop smoking. Maybe you're burning the candle at both ends, and need to slow down, delegate. For a more in-depth analysis of your health, refer to your Mansion of Health.

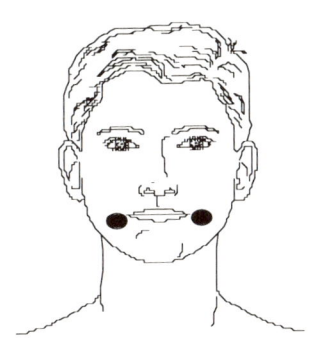

### The Mansions of Assets

These mansions are located between your brows and your eyelids. They are linked to your Mansions of the Home in that the mansion on the left tells you about your home (or a home that you are hoping to get) and the mansion on the right is concerned with the property inside your home. Check these mansions before you begin any home improvements, or make any investments.

A firm, smooth, and well-covered mansion indicates that your plans will run smoothly, and that you are being wise with your money and property. Alternatively, should the mansions be bloated or noticeably hollow and blemished, you should think carefully before making any big decisions. Consider seeking professional advice.

Bear in mind that the mansion on the left is also connected to property coming to you through your father and that the mansion on the right signifies incoming property from your mother and her side of the family.

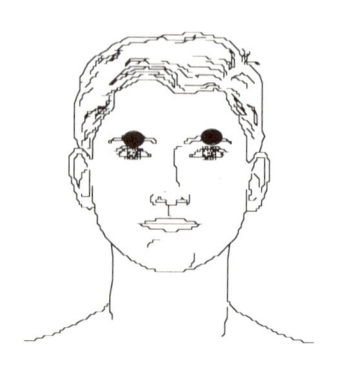

### The Mansion of Riches

Have you ever heard someone being described as having a nose for money? Well, there is a good reason behind this saying. This mansion is located on the tip of your nose. It tells you about your present and future financial prospects.

You would be prudent to check this point before agreeing to or finalizing any financial transaction such as borrowing, lending, or requesting a raise. Ideally, this mansion should be of a good color – preferably the same tone as the rest of your face. If this is the case, you can be confident that you are getting a fair deal, or making a good investment – or that you simply have a sensible balance between income and expenditure. Your current actions bode well for your future financial stability.

If this mansion has too much color and (providing you don't have a cold!) if it is noticeably darker than the rest of your face, then you need to take stock. Are you being too extravagant and wasting your money? Resist the temptation to extend your overdraft this month; leave your credit card at home this shopping trip; perhaps further investigation is needed before you risk your hard-earned cash on those shares. Keep an eye on your purse-strings for the moment: forewarned is forearmed!

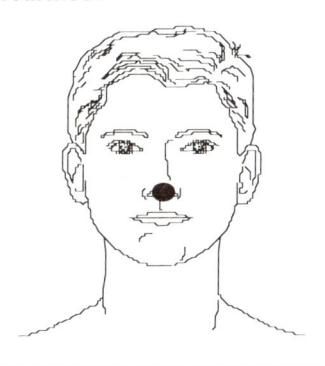

# THE PROFILE OF THE FOREHEAD

TERRAIN – MOUNTAIN
VITAL ENERGY – ACTIVITY
FATE – ADVENTURE
PLANET – MARS
MILESTONE OF LIFE – FIRST (15-31 YEARS OF AGE)
FACIAL MANSIONS:
* THE MANSION OF LIFE
* THE MANSIONS OF PARENTS
* THE MANSIONS OF MOVING
* THE MANSION OF SUCCESS
* THE MANSIONS OF BROTHERS, SISTERS, AND FRIENDS
* THE MANSIONS OF JOY AND LUCK

**THE FOREHEAD**

The forehead symbolizes relationships with your parents and family; the amount of support they gave you, and also the values they instilled in you. The top outer corners of the forehead contain bones that are connected directly to your parents. Ideally, these bones are fairly prominent (without protruding too much), which means that you are highly intelligent, and have received a lot of support and mental stimulation from your parents. The things that your parents gave you affect your chances of achievement and your attitude toward success. These two things are obviously also affected by your own intelligence and ambition.

When deciding on the shape of your forehead, try to imagine it without hair! In other words, you shouldn't use your hairline as a guide for determining the shape. When examining your forehead, you also have to consider its height (high, medium, or low), along with its profile.

A high forehead implies that you have a good relationship with your parents and other family members. If you are not the first and oldest child, the chances are that you will have to care for your parents in some way. A forehead of medium height also points to good family relationships and a good level of intelligence. A low forehead is less fortunate, as it signals a weak relationship and poor parental support. This could lead to some kind of psychological trouble.

It also pays to look at the lines on your forehead. One horizontal line situated high on your forehead indicates that success *will* be achieved in life. If this line sits low on your forehead, then a moderate amount of success is to be expected if you continue with your current course in life. Two lines are the mark of a brilliant mind and a person who is determined, ambitious and a high achiever. Three lines show an individual who has a huge amount of luck, without necessarily being particularly smart. This person is definitely standing underneath the smiling star of success.

Another point for consideration is this: if you have a mole in the middle of your forehead, it signifies that you have the ability to do well in your professional life. This doesn't necessarily mean that you will find happiness and success in your personal relationships. To achieve this, you must learn how to compromise.

There are three different forehead shapes, along with four types of forehead profiles.

## THE THREE FOREHEAD SHAPES

### The Rounded Forehead

If you have a high rounded forehead, you have a happy history, with a good, stable family life and childhood. Although you are intelligent, your parents never really encouraged you to be ambitious or to be a high achiever. You are an even-tempered individual, who isn't particularly competitive. Chances are that you're not hugely ambitious, and that you'll be content with a "normal" life. You don't strive for any kind of glamour or high status; you're quite settled, no matter what life brings you. If your forehead is low, you haven't had the most positive of upbringings, and you didn't get all the support you may have wanted. This is not to say that you can't have a great future, so long as you put enough effort into your life.

## The Narrow Forehead

This type of forehead, whether high or of medium height, shows that you are spontaneous and adventurous. This is balanced, thankfully, with a good measure of intelligence and common sense. Should this forehead be low, the gift of common sense is missing (or at least it's underdeveloped), which means that you can easily get in trouble. You aren't in control of your impulses, and you're constantly finding yourself in sticky situations. You would have a better chance of success if you could learn to be less impetuous.

## The Square Forehead

A high, square forehead shows that you are very intelligent and have a well-balanced personality. You are a fortunate individual with the firm foundation of a strong family. If your square forehead is of medium height, you have a good amount of common sense and initiative. Rest assured that you will achieve a good level of success. A low, square forehead means that although you have suffered from various disadvantages, you have a positive character, and are capable and practical.

## THE FOUR TYPES OF FOREHEAD PROFILE

### The Straight Profile
You're an intelligent person who could go far. You use your strong will and determination to achieve your goals. But these qualities are liable to turn into stubbornness. You have to make sure that you don't let yourself become too rigid or pedantic. You must be able to adapt; otherwise, you could hold yourself back in life. If your forehead is low with a straight profile, you need to be prepared to put a lot of effort into your earlier life in order to succeed in your later life.

### The Sloping Profile
Nobody would dream of calling you a stick-in-the-mud! You love to have fun and do things on the spur of the moment, without thought or advance planning. However, you really should develop a sense of consequence, and start to realize that adventurous activities can lead to unnecessary trouble. Find a balance – have fun (it's what life's all about!), but also learn how to exercise sense and restraint at times.

### The Rounded Profile
Spontaneity is your middle name and you like to have fun, but you're not naturally a thoughtless or reckless person. You like to stick to safe and sensible boundaries, without limiting your lifestyle. Your strength means that you're not easily influenced or persuaded to take unnecessary risks by the people around you. You're very adaptable, and you're able to cope with any unexpected event that crops up in your life.

**The Protruding Profile**

This type of profile almost seems to balloon out from the hairline; it's very distinct. It's a sign of mega-intelligence, with the ambition to match. The trouble is that such intelligence is often accompanied by high-mindedness, and you may well lose sight of reality. You need to make sure that this doesn't happen. If you stay grounded, you should be able to reach great heights of success. This could make you happy, just as long as you get to have all the luxuries in life, too!

# THE PROFILE OF THE EARS

**THE LEFT EAR**
TERRAIN – RIVER
VITAL ENERGY – PROGRESSING & LEARNING
FATE – WISDOM
PLANET - JUPITER
MILESTONE OF LIFE – NONE (1-7 YEARS OF AGE)
FACIAL MANSIONS - NONE

**THE RIGHT EAR**
TERRAIN – RIVER
VITAL ENERGY – GRACE & ELEGANCE
FATE – STATUS
PLANET - VENUS
MILESTONE OF LIFE – NONE (8-14 YEARS OF AGE)
FACIAL MANSIONS – NONE

**THE EARS**
The ears are one of the main facial traits to be examined. They reveal truths about your character, and in turn, your chances of success in life. It is possible to look at the ears of a child and predict what kind of personality traits he or she will have in adulthood – excluding, of course, outside influences and experiences.

When looking at the ears, make sure that you consider their size, position, set, color and form. So long as the ears are well formed, large ears bode well for a successful life – especially if they are long. Combined with good shape, small ears show a relatively high level of life potential. Long, floppy, protruding ears indicate laziness and even carelessness – characteristics that can hold you back in life.

If your ears are positioned high (the top of the ears level with or above the eyebrows), it shows an intellectual mind with success being reached in the early stages of life. Ears of medium position (the top of the ears reaching between the eyelids and eyebrows), it signifies a responsible and hard-working individual who will achieve a moderate level of success. If your ears are positioned low (top of the ears drawing level with the eyes), success can be achieved, but a distaste for work and a somewhat lazy disposition must be overcome first.

Protruding ears show that you are a laid-back and lackadaisical individual who can be careless and sometimes clumsy. Close-set ears indicate that you are a balanced individual with common sense and a well-rounded personality. Finally, tight-set ears show that you may be self-restricting due to a lack of daring, and an approach to life that goes beyond what is sensible.

If your ears are the same color as your face, or are lighter than your face, you have the perfect tone. This shows that you can reach a good level of success and achievement. Should your ears be red or darker than your face, it shows that you have an unbalanced temperament and that you are an individual who is prone to outbursts of anger that could hinder advancement.

The ideal lobe is not joined to the side of the head. It is soft, full (but not too fleshy), nicely rounded, neither too red nor too pale. Long and fleshy lobes denote a wise and knowledgeable individual. Lobes that are attached to the side of the head show a self-centered and somewhat selfish individual who is preoccupied with attaining personal goals to the detriment of everyone else.

Secrets of the FACE

The form of the ears depends greatly on the **Inner and Outer Wheels**.

The **outer wheel** is the rim of cartilage around the edge of the ear.

**A very thick outer wheel:** This shows an individual who is more concerned with the physical being than spiritual awareness – possibly to the extent of sexual excess.

**A thin outer wheel:** This indicates a self-centered, selfish individual. He or she tends to form relationships only with those who can be useful in some way.

**A pointed outer wheel:** Again, this signals an exploitative individual who is not above stepping on others in order to be successful. This person may be irresponsible and cannot always be trusted.

The **inner wheel** is the piece of cartilage forming a kind of shelf around the ear cavity.

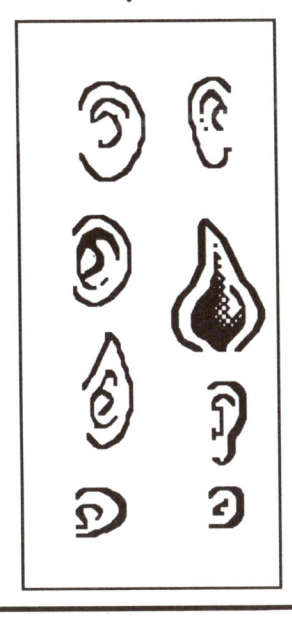

**A shapely inner wheel:** This indicates a balanced, emotionally stable individual.
**A protruding inner wheel:** This belongs to the sociable extrovert who dislikes being alone.
**A flat inner wheel:** This shows an introverted individual who rejects other people's company and who tends to keep all thoughts and feelings inside.

Any kind of mole on either of your ears is considered a fortunate sign. You will be lucky, and will do well in all areas of your life.

## THE SEVEN EAR TYPES

### Large Ears

As a child, large ears may be a source of misery and are often the butt of cruel jokes and jibes. However, according to this ancient Chinese art, large ears are an asset. Combined with good shape, positioning and color, big ears mean big ideas that are put into good practice, and lead to financial and professional success. These undertakings bring rewards that last throughout your lifetime. This type of ear also indicates your ability to be a good listener; you listen to all sides of the stories you are told. You are outgoing and socially aware. Your goodwill and even-tempered character are valuable to you along the path to success.

### Large Ears with Protruding Inner Wheels

This ear indicates adventure, action and aura. You won't be found in a quiet country village, lazing in bed, or glued to the TV all day! Your high energy levels demand constant action. You love to travel and meet as many people as possible. Your determination and daring (with a little help from your friends!) constitutes your recipe for success.

Your charisma and sociability mean that you are not suited to a regular profession or a mundane office job. Instead you will find your vocation in a more unusual and exciting occupation.

**Large Ears with Long Lobes**

If you have ears of this type, all of the qualities of the large ear apply to you. You are also blessed with a philosophical approach to life. Long lobes indicate that others will often approach you for counsel on spiritual matters – or just for a shoulder to cry on.

Deferred gratification tends to replace instant success, but when you *do* make it, be assured that you will reach great heights and gain the respect of many.

If this isn't your ear type and you're reading this analysis with someone else in mind, take note! Before placing your well-being in the hands of the so-called wise, check the other ear characteristics to make sure that you don't fall prey to a charlatan!

**A Rounded Lobeless Ear**

You are fun-loving and sociable with a good-sized compassionate heart. These qualities mean that you have a natural magnetism. You live for the moment and it is unlikely that you make any kind of concrete provision for your future. But have no fear! You are naturally equipped to deal with the unexpected emergencies that occur in life; your innate ability to cope in a crisis carries you through these trouble-spots.

To others, it seems that Lady Luck is always at your side, and it's likely that your career will skyrocket (you're always in the right place at the right time). If luck alone isn't enough, you can be sure that your open disposition will bring you plenty of friends who will lend you a helping hand.

**Shell-Shaped Ears with a Large Hollow**

You are an extrovert who loves to socialize, and you're not particularly keen on being alone. Your open mind (indicated by the large hollow) means that people often come to you to confess their secrets – they know you won't judge them. Your love of gossip, however, means that their secrets won't remain safe for very long!

If you have this ear type without a lobe, you are very hospitable and like to entertain in the comfort of your own home. You live for the present and are very much into what's "in."

If you have a protruding inner wheel, you are an extrovert in the extreme and you like to put your energy to good use – helping others. A flat inner wheel indicates that communication is of utmost importance to you. From the mass media to a daily gossip session with your neighbor, you have your finger on the pulse of society and you know who is doing what, where, when, and with whom!

**Small, Shapely Ears**

If this is your ear type, then you are a lover of security, stability, organization, and beautiful surroundings. You are a warm, artistic and graceful individual, who will achieve success in the middle stages of your life. This success will be achieved through honest hard work and your adherence to the usual rules and channels of the workplace. You are often blessed with a well-ordered and peaceful life.

However, your need to conform can, in later years, become problematic. As you grow older, you may become set in your ways, finding it increasingly difficult to adapt to different circumstances and situations.

As long as you are given the opportunity to express yourself freely, you will be happy with even a small amount of success.

**Pointy Ears**

Your playful and energetic personality means that you are no stranger to popularity. People are drawn to you by your mischievous nature. You also have a tendency to be an opportunist; once you've got what you want, you move on without so much as a backward glance (this is not done maliciously or even consciously, though). Reliability is not your strong point.

If your pointy ear is also large with a well-formed lobe, your innate intelligence enables you to make your way through life with great success, despite a lack of definite goals and concentrated focus.

A liking for quick and easy money may steer you towards the world of gambling – or some other kind of tricky business. Your innovative side means that despite the risks you take, your chances of success in life are high.

# THE PROFILE OF THE EYES

**THE RIGHT EYE**
TERRAIN – RIVER
VITAL ENERGY – CREATIVITY
FATE – INTELLIGENCE
MILESTONE OF LIFE – SECOND (31-50 YEARS OF AGE)
FACIAL MANSION – THE PALACE OF ASSETS:
YIN / FEMININE ENERGIES

**THE LEFT EYE**
TERRAIN – RIVER
VITAL ENERGY – CREATIVITY
FATE – INTELLIGENCE
MILESTONE OF LIFE – SECOND (31-50 YEARS OF AGES)
FACIAL MANSION – THE MANSION OF ASSETS:
YANG / MASCULINE ENERGIES

## THE EYES

The eyes have long been called the windows of the soul. By looking someone in the eye, we can see their true inner emotions and feelings. Eye contact is one of the most powerful tools of non-verbal communication that humans possess. Looking someone directly in the eye can convey integrity, truth, attentiveness and also attraction.

When examining your own or someone else's eyes, there are a number of factors you must consider: the size, setting, and color. Ideally the eyes should be large and open. This shows a creative person who is socially and personally aware. The large eye sees all sides of any argument or situation, and this means that their owner is not likely to jump to any hasty decision or conclusion.

## COLOR
Ideally, the **whites of the eyes** should be clear, clean and bright. If they are tinged with yellow, red or any other color, it is a sign of low energy levels, and more care needs to be taken. Check your diet, exercise habits and general life-style.

**Dark brown irises:** These show a person who is energetic and mentally active.
**Green irises:** An individual who is interested in philosophy and the mysteries of life.
**Blue irises:** A happy and jovial individual. These qualities are proportionate to the depth and richness of color.

## POSITION
**Close-set eyes:** This indicates people who never really take charge of their own lives. Instead they remain dependent on their parents and families. If they are not careful, they will not develop an open mind and independent train of thought.

**Wide-set eyes:** This indicates people who are separated from their families. It may be possible that they deliberately turned their back on their families and everything the latter stood for. This emotional distance means that the people in question have become power-hungry.

**Evenly-spaced eyes:** (a width of one eye between the two eyes) These are people who have a healthy and balanced relationship with their parents and families. This, in turn, points to a well-balanced personality.

## THE SEVEN BASIC EYE TYPES

Beside the seven basic eye types described below, there are a further four types that are more unusual. They are characterized by their amazing gaze. When you come across these eyes, you'll know it; their piercing power will seem to cut through to your very soul.

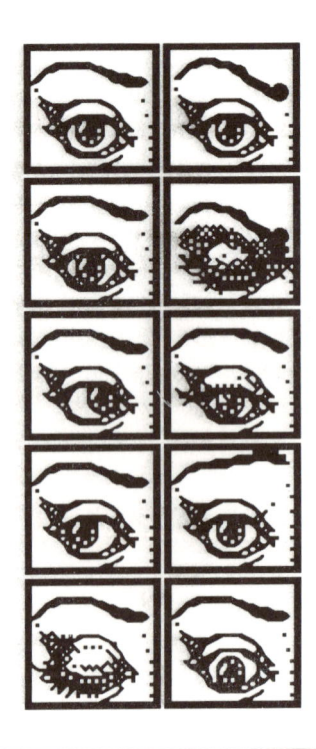

### Big Eyes
You are an extrovert who is open and honest. Your intelligence and sensitivity combine to form excellent leadership qualities. Big eyes reflect good observational skills, which means that you notice the small aspects of life. The sexy sparkle in your eyes often attracts the attention of others, and you are not short of admirers or lovers.

Your ability to focus your mental energies (which are quite considerable) means that you can reach great heights. One of the most enjoyable and successful periods of your life is in your mid- to late thirties, when nothing can hold you back.

### Big Eyes, Small Irises
In this eye type, the white of the eye is easily seen below the iris (the colored part of the eye). You are reluctant to conform, and prefer to do your own thing; some even call you rebellious! You're dissatisfied with your lot in life and are always wanting more – or just something different. You are constantly on the move in an attempt to find that something which is missing from your life (even if this "something" is actually nothing). You move from one relationship to the next or one job to another, never really allowing enough time for love to blossom or promotion to occur. If you could only control your restlessness, who knows what might happen? You're not particularly fond of responsibility, either, and have a tendency to pass the buck.

As you make your way through life, you need to exercise some caution as regards the people you meet and befriend. You tend to attract the kind of people who can hinder and hold you back in life. Your generous nature makes you an easy target for them, and they may take advantage of you and exert a negative influence on your life.

From your mid- to late thirties, you would be well advised to learn how to hold your ground and develop staying power. By continuing your haphazard and disruptive ways, you'll only lurch from crisis to crisis, causing you to pick up and run time after time. Learn how to exercise forbearance in the face of adversity (or conformity!) – don't give up at the slightest provocation. Use your latent energy to capitalize on the opportunities that come your way, instead of fueling an unwarranted feeling of discontent and endless yearning.

**Deep-set Eyes**
Remember the saying, "Still waters run deep"? Well, this certainly applies to this eye type. You are an intellectual but romantic dreamer who has a highly developed practical side. Even though you are a great thinker and philosopher, you do have you feet on the ground – well, one of them, anyway!

If you are not financially independent at the moment, you can be sure that the time will come when you will be able to provide for yourself and your family.

Your thoughtful nature means that you don't rush into anything in an impulsive manner. To others, you are a romantic fool, whose head is floating in the stars. You may be subject to the criticism of others who make fun of your high-minded ways. What these people don't understand, though, is that you are sensitive and take any insult to heart. Any hurt that you feel is internalized and not expressed freely.

You are often sought out by those in some kind of emotional difficulty. People with worries or problems come to you for counsel; your incredibly open mind mulls over the troubles of others, finding unusual and unorthodox solutions. Where many minds have failed, yours will probably succeed. You can expect to become more grounded when you reach your mid-thirties.

**Small Eyes**

Once you get to the point of trusting a person and forming a bond with them, everything is plain sailing. But getting there is not always easy. You can be extremely difficult to get to know. You can be overly defensive (even when it's not necessary) and somewhat untrusting of people. Learn to give people a chance and don't be too quick to ridicule or judge harshly.

You tend to limit yourself in life; you are aware of your abilities, but never push yourself beyond them. You are content with your skills and don't seek to improve them in order to take yourself to a higher plane. Sometimes though, you may become conceited, believing that you are better than you actually are. Make sure you expand your mind and develop a wider view of life.

You are sometimes too hard on yourself. Self-criticism can be useful, but if taken to far, it can actually be destructive. It is likely that your mid-thirties will see you becoming a perfectionist in the extreme. Remember that the pursuit of perfection is natural, but it can be damaging to the psyche if taken too far.

**Bulging Eyes**

You are a strong-willed extrovert. While you can be impulsive, you are not blindly foolish. If the going is good, you will move forward with your plans. You will also put them on hold, if necessary. The wisdom and insight you have imply that most of the ventures you embark upon in your life will have a successful outcome. Your charisma draws people to you. Your compassion and desire to help them through hard times means you are never short of friends.

You are amazingly adaptable and somewhat of a chameleon; you are able to completely change your life in the blink of an eye. You tend to make some kind of sweeping change quite often.

You find it hard to resist any offer that comes your way – from a change in the direction of your career, to the invitation from that gorgeous girl or guy you met in the bar last week. The fact that you feel little responsibility toward anything or anyone doesn't help matters. Where others see unnecessary risks and gambles, you see an opportunity not to be missed. Even if you lose, you pick yourself up and carry on.

When you reach your mid-thirties, it is likely that you will also have reached a comfortable (and above average) position in life. You will probably be faced with some sort of endeavor that you'll find hard to resist; and you'll be tempted to risk everything you've achieved for this "one last" offer. Just think before you act.

**Eyes that Turn Upward**

You are an energetic and cheerful character. Your sense of humor means that it's fun to be around you. Being an animated conversationalist also helps you in the popularity stakes. Another attractive quality of yours is the fact that you always look on the bright side of life; you are ever the optimist.

Your energy and enthusiasm for life disguises the fact that you have a short fuse and are prone to losing your temper – even when it's not wholly warranted. You find it difficult to maintain a long-term love affair. Partners are initially attracted by your joviality, and everything runs smoothly as long as you are getting exactly what you want. However, the second your every want or whim is not met, the temperature drops, the fun ends, and you subject your loved one to tantrums or the silent treatment.

This lack of stability is echoed in your work ethic. You are happiest in an ever-changing environment where you will not be tempted to stray into looking for another job after the first week, and where you can fulfill your social side and mingle with a variety of personalities. You are simply not suited to staid or monotonous positions where your work goes unnoticed.

As you approach your forties, your temperament will become more stable; allowing you to forge ahead successfully both in love and business.

**Eyes that Point Downward**

Your love and consideration knows no bounds and you are always willing to sympathize and empathize with those in emotional turmoil. You often put others' needs and well-being before your own, but you must be sure to exercise some caution. Others may spot your kind-heartedness and take advantage of it. Your dislike for speaking up and defending yourself (you might upset someone) means that you are sometimes treated like a doormat. This is a huge shame because you really do have a heart of gold and a beautiful soul.

You are particularly vulnerable in matters of affection. You often form attachments with unsuitable partners who sometime purposely prey on your good points. At other times, it is your unquenchable desire to help that gets you into trouble. You may be drawn to problematic personalities in the belief that you can help or change them. You fail to realize that it is impossible to help someone who is unwilling to help themselves. The result is that you could be pulled down, drained not only of your energy, but also of your self-esteem and your belief in yourself.

However, be confident that experience is a good teacher and that your mid-thirties will be a benchmark in your love life. It is around that age that you will finally win the true love of someone who appreciates your inner warmth and full value.

## UNUSUAL EYE TYPES

### Tiger's Eyes
These round eyes are characterized by gorgeous gold speckles in the irises. You have a strong and frank personality, which can manifest itself in an overly blunt and harsh manner. If unchecked, this can alienate those you care for most. Expect to accumulate financial wealth in your forties (probably as a result of working in a high-status job).

### Cow Eyes
These huge eyes are framed by beautiful, long, thick lashes. You have a tranquil and easy disposition, and you are incredibly patient. You are hardworking and more than able to bear responsibility. You think carefully before making any decision or change in your life. Your pacifying aura means that you are easy and amiable to be around – a person without friction or tension.

### Cat's Eyes

These eyes glisten with a yellow or green gleam. You share some of the cat's feline traits: you are alert, agile, and luxury-loving. You must be sure though, that your love of all good things doesn't develop into self-indulgence. Your ambitions will be realized as you move from your thirties into your forties.

### Elephant Eyes

These eyes are very broad. A line beneath them creates a ridge of skin that forms a little bag. Like an elephant, you are strong, yet gentle. You have an enormous capacity to love and you thoroughly enjoy socializing. There is one sure way to provoke your peaceful nature, however: if you or any of those you care about are threatened in any way and your anger is roused, you will charge the perpetrator with the formidable force of the animal that gives this eye type its name.

## THE SIGNIFICANCE OF LINES AROUND YOUR EYES

We all know what "crow's feet" are, and most of us dread the appearance of these lines at the outer corners of our eyes. We see them as a sign that heralds the advent of the aging process. These lines have separate significance according to which eye they are near to.

At the outer corner of the left eye, the number of lines you have correspond with the number of marriage (or marriage-like) relationships you will have. The number of lines around the corner of your right eye tells you about the number of adulterous affairs or "indiscretions" that you will have in your time. This is a particularly interesting eye to consider when you're looking at the face of a potential partner!

Horizontal lines on the eyelids are good signs, but more than one line either above or below your eyes shows someone who has trouble trusting people. If you want to befriend a person, check this area first. If the lines are crooked, then you're meeting an individual who is friendly and giving – you'll just have to work that little bit harder to prove your good intentions before they will even consider letting their guard down.

## THE EYEBROWS

Your eyebrows frame your face. Their importance in creating an image can be seen in the number of hours that women spend plucking and shaping them.

The eyebrows reveal the special skills you possess which, if properly utilized, will lead you toward success and fame. The eyebrows also illustrate areas of ability that will help you develop a good and well-respected name for yourself. In addition, they indicate aspects of your personality – particularly how you behave within relationships (professional and personal).

Some personality traits are signified by the eyebrows and are not influenced by shape.

Smooth, shapely eyebrows indicate a person who is well-balanced, loyal, and nice to be around.

Prominent and heavy eyebrows show an active and powerful personality.

Thin, sparse eyebrows indicate an individual who is flexible and congenial in all kinds of relationships.

Long protruding hairs presage a long life.

Untidy brows indicate sexual instability.

Straggly hairs at the outer tip of the eyebrows symbolize many good friendships and also the assistance given to you throughout your lifetime by these friends.

The space between your eyebrows contains the magic "Third Eye" (see the Facial Mansions). A light-colored mole here is a lucky thing; it bodes well for your future career and it also indicates an open mind. Throughout your lifetime experiences, you will develop a broad world-view, and you will fully understand that there is more to life than that which is in your immediate surroundings.

As with the eyes, there are seven basic eyebrow types. In addition to this, there are five unusual types of eyebrows.

## THE SEVEN BASIC EYEBROW TYPES

### Arched Eyebrows

This type is the epitome of the ideal eyebrow. It symbolizes the ultimate in feminine beauty and is the pinnacle of masculine good looks.

You are artistic and creative – qualities which complement your romantic side. While you're not averse to romance, you have a well-balanced mind, and nobody can accuse you of being a dreamer. You are fair and just, and exercise discipline without being overly zealous. You are also extremely self-controlled.

The above qualities mean that you are able to reach a high position in whatever field you choose, and you can expect to be well respected.

### Curved Eyebrows

The accentuated curve of these eyebrows allows more space for the Mansions of Assets; they emphasize the role that possessions will play in your life – in this case, the important role that they will play in your career. You will probably be involved either in property management or retailing – anything to do with making money.

You have strong ambitions and are a highly focused individual. This a good combination for making money. The fact that you are a good judge of character also helps you; you can cleverly adapt your sales technique to suit anyone you have to deal with. All of this means you have a very promising career.

Your stable mind allows you to forge firm friendships, alliances, and partnerships. But you do have a tendency to become overly domineering. You tend to forget that personal relationships involve two sides equally. You may be the main breadwinner, but that doesn't give you *carte blanche* to throw your weight around at home and lord it over your loved ones. Resist the temptation to manipulate and control others. It would be a good idea to keep your personal life completely separate from your professional life.

You may be the company owner, managing director, or office supervisor during work hours, but at home you can't expect your family to serve you as your employees or co-workers are paid to do. Remember that your family are people, not possessions.

### Bent Eyebrows

These eyebrows have a flat underside with the top forming a stout triangular shape. Adventure, action and drama are your catch-phrases. Where others see a problem, you see only a challenge – something to be conquered and overcome rather than feared.

You tend to veer toward some kind of risky business. It could be investment banking, playing the stock exchange, or even gambling at the blackjack tables of the most glamorous casinos. Whatever path you take, you can be sure that you will find success, and possibly your slice of fame, through some sort of precarious pursuit.

Others see your active attitude to life (the way you take the bull by the horns and shake it violently!), and they come to you for help when they are going through hard times. They hope that some of your vitality will rub off on them. If this is to happen, it had better happen quickly; you don't stick around for long.

You're always on the move, which doesn't make for good concrete relationships. Your tireless need for constant change and variety means that you only offer instability and that you may even be prone to promiscuity.

### Ascending Eyebrows

You are dignified and self-confident. You're also extremely ambitious and as far as you're concerned, the sky is your only limit. And you'll go higher than that if you get your own way! Such determination to reach your desired goals means that you can be inconsiderate in your dealings with others. You're not above trampling those around you underfoot in order to reach the next rung on the ladder.

Once you have climbed to the top, you must be certain that you treat those below you with the respect they deserve. Make sure you don't let authority go to your head. After all, you don't want to be known as a tyrant!

You love to travel and you want to see, feel and experience everything that there is in life. You are acutely aware that there's a huge world out there, and one of your many missions is to explore (or conquer?) the globe.

Learn how to combine this independent travel-bug of yours with consideration for others. Doing this will help you to build and uphold healthy, happy and balanced relationships.

### Descending Eyebrows

While you may look weak, helpless and forlorn, you are actually quite the opposite. Drawn to you by your apparent vulnerability, others often help you in some way, even if you don't actually need any help.

You may be tempted to play on this, acting as a victim to gain the support of others. Try not to do so. Remember that you will feel most rewarded by achieving your goals through your own efforts. You are not actively aggressive or outgoing, but you do manage to get things done in a roundabout sort of way.

Some people find helplessness (real or imagined) very attractive. Your natural sexiness combines with this to make quite a seductive cocktail. You would do well to develop a strategy whereby you can exercise your true strength to its full potential.

You're likely to find success and gain respect through

working in the arts. Whether you're creating a masterpiece, writing a rhapsody or opening your own art gallery, be confident in your own abilities; don't rely on the unfounded and unnecessary sympathies of others. Try to avoid getting embroiled in situations which could be harmful to your reputation.

**Horizontal Eyebrows**
You are physically and mentally strong. You are also straightforward, and have a good deal of common sense. You're not content with a mundane and monotonous daily life. Instead, you prefer challenges that keep you on your toes and utilize your mental energies. Did I forget to mention that fact that you also enjoy being in control of everything you do?

Women with this type of eyebrow generally eschew a life of pure domesticity, choosing instead an alternative source of more exciting work outside of the home.

Whether male or female, you perform excellently in managerial positions where your natural intelligence, capabilities, and sense are allowed to prevail. However, if you are not careful, you will become inconsiderate (even if you don't mean to be). Consumed with the desire to be as successful as possible, you may forget to show compassion and understanding toward your co-workers.

This lack of compassion and warmth may also be seen in your personal relationships. You are in the habit of preserving a distance between yourself and those you should really be striving to be close to. Within the family you can become standoffish, choosing to let others care for your loved ones, which in turn frees you to concentrate on your professional life. Personal relationships may become strained and tense – your partner may be unable to come to terms with your emotional distance and seeming coldness, and may have trouble dealing with your domineering ways.

**Short Eyebrows**

You are an incredibly ambitious and determined individual, which means that you are likely to reach your goals at an earlier-than-average age. You value your independence and go to great lengths to hang on to it. This means that you're constantly driving yourself onward and upward. Your sheer determination enables you to overcome any obstacle in your path: the higher the wall, the harder you climb.

You are a fast and astute thinker and when a quick and clever decision needs to be made, you are more than able to rise to the occasion.

You don't like to waste time, preferring to get straight to the point; you don't see any need for beating around the bush. Sometimes though, you are too blunt and blatant. Harsh words wound even when said without malicious intent. You need to learn how to control your short temper, and you could also benefit from studying the social skills of diplomacy and tact.

You can be amazingly passionate when it comes to love. At the beginning of a new romance your chosen one may not know what's hit them as they are swept away by your fiery emotions. But this intense feeling doesn't always last, and if it fades, you quickly move on.

## UNUSUAL EYEBROWS

### Thin Crescent Eyebrows
Picture the shape of a new moon and you have the shape of these eyebrows. They look fragile and give you a slightly superficial and shallow appearance. In actual fact, though, you are a genuine person with a kind and calm nature. You like to nurture those you care for. This trait probably stems from your upbringing, which you may have shared with a large family in a happy and stable atmosphere. When you have a problem, you remain calm and think through your options. You're not prone to bouts of blind panic. Besides, things always seem to work out for you.

### Thick Crescent Eyebrows
These eyebrows are thick at the bridge of the nose and trail off into a thin outer tip. You are sociable and thoroughly enjoy mixing with lots of people – especially if they're powerful and well respected. You have good communication skills that you utilize in your career. The connections you make through your gatherings with the rich and powerful will aid you in furthering your career. Bear in mind, though, that great success will not be yours until you reach your forties.

### United Eyebrows
Have you ever thought of plucking away the hairs that unite your eyebrows? Well, maybe you should! This would help to diffuse your red-hot temper. You can sometimes be overly aggressive, and you are suited to positions where controlled levels of aggression can be used (judiciously, of course). Authoritative occupations appeal to you, and you

will do well in such jobs just as long as you are able to exercise self-control, and don't let power go to your head.

### Willowy Eyebrows

These long and elegantly curved eyebrows extend delicately toward the outer corner of the eye. You are intelligent, alert, and more than a little bit romantic. There is a chance that your intelligence could develop into an overly intellectual mind with a purely theoretical view of and approach to life. Try to make sure that you don't become superficial and shallow; otherwise you could earn yourself a name for being an untrustworthy individual in both your personal and professional relationships.

### Lionine Eyebrows

These eyebrows are prominent and heavy. Their fullness gives you a stern appearance that may deter people from approaching you in the belief that you're a fierce and hard individual; they're completely wrong, but it's their loss!

In reality you're a big softie! You're very gentle, loving, and affectionate. It's because of these qualities that you are able to form strong friendships and openly loving relationships. You truly have a heart of gold. Having said that, you're not beyond being cruel to be kind, or attacking a wrong-doer in order to protect those closest to you.

## THE SIGNIFICANCE OF LINES AROUND YOUR EYEBROWS

One vertical line between your eyebrows is not a particularly fortunate marking. It shows that pressures and problems may plague you and that, although you are quick off the mark, you're unlikely to win many races. Your chances of success depend more on your determination and will power than on your unquestionable intelligence. Don't despair, though: you can succeed just as long as you don't give up – success always smells sweetest after a struggle!

The usual marking here is two vertical lines. This is nothing out of the ordinary, and is certainly *not* an unlucky sign.

To have three lines between your eyebrows is a sign of great intelligence and insight, which you will use to obtain a good level of success. Three lines is a very fortunate marking.

Bear in mind that to have more than three lines between your eyebrows is quite unfortunate. More than three lines suggests that you need to focus your energies in order to be able to attain success.

A horizontal line between the eyebrows points to a domineering individual who needs to learn the meaning of humility and tolerance. The more horizontal lines there are, the more conspicuous this is.

# THE PROFILE OF THE NOSE

TERRAIN – MOUNTAIN
VITAL ENERGY – TRANQUILLITY
FATE – SECURITY
PLANET – SATURN
MILESTONE OF LIFE – SECOND (31-50 YEARS OF AGE)
FACIAL MANSIONS – THE MANSION OF HEALTH
THE MANSION OF RICHES

### THE NOSE

The nose represents achievement and the attendant rewards that you can expect to enjoy from your forties onward. Your nose can give you information about your career path, and how personality traits are helping or hindering your progress and advancement.

You can also find out about your attitude to money by examining your nose. Are you like a squirrel, hoarding and saving each penny until your bank balance blossoms? Maybe you never have any money to spare because you just spend, spend, spend! Ideally though, you are one of those people who saves sensibly while still enjoying yourself.

When looking at your own or another person's nose, you should consider the color, the root, the bridge, and also the tip. Ideally the nose should be the same color as the rest of the face.

If your nose is red, it signifies overindulgence and a short, fiery temper. A pale or white nose shows diminished levels of energy or even an illness. But please don't be alarmed if this should apply to your coloring at this time!

Ideally, the root of the nose is smooth, unblemished and a pink color. All of this would imply that you have the right

## Secrets of the FACE

amount of energy and positivity to take yourself forward and achieve your chosen goals. A concave root is not particularly fortunate for business dealings. A flat and wide root signifies that a reasonable level of success will be reached. A convex root means that you can be sure that your career will be highly successful and that you will be the recipient of people's respect.

The bridge of your nose must also be examined. A straight bridge indicates a high energy level that is conducive to reaching your full potential. A thin and bony bridge denotes that you are sometimes too critical of both yourself and those around you in your pursuit of perfection. You need to learn to consider other people's feelings in order to increase your chances of success. A thin and pointed bridge means that money and wealth won't fall into your lap; you'll have to work hard for it. A flat bridge means that you should be prepared to work hard for a moderate level of recognition and success.

The tip of your nose should preferably be round without being too fleshy. This is certainly the best tip to have. The nose represents masculine energies, and also the male reproductive organs. If a man has a mole on the tip of his nose, it is a sign of high fertility levels, and it also signifies that he may have many children.

In total there are eleven different nose types. Seven of these are regular shapes, and the remaining four are more unusual.

## THE SEVEN BASIC NOSE TYPES

### The Straight Nose
You are an honest and trustworthy person. Your balanced temperament means that you usually speak only the truth. You have a visible inner energy and are pleasant to be around. You are not judgmental, and like to give everyone a fair chance; you are extremely tolerant.

Success is no stranger to you and it seems to come into your life easily. People don't realize that you work hard for your rewards, though. You rely on your courage and determination to get you through. The fact is, you have a large measure of initiative and an active eye for business. Once you've identified your target, nothing deflects you from your carefully plotted course, and you undoubtedly get what you want. Your focused approach to life helps you build up quite a nice record of achievement!

### The Pug Nose
You have a happy-go-lucky nature and no time for convention. You make many friends, as you're such fun to be with, and you have a special sparkle, too. You are considerate of others, and when it's needed, you often receive the help and assistance of those who care about you.

You are known to be a generous person, but this can sometimes get you in trouble. Money burns a hole in your pocket, so you probably find yourself a little bit short of cash from time to time. This isn't helped by the fact that you find it a bit tricky to hold down a job for any length of time. It's an undeniable and unavoidable fact that rules and routine just don't suit you. You prefer to go your own way, and sometimes your boss is happy to let you do exactly that!

Just as the tip of your nose points skyward, so do your ideas. Your view of reality sometimes gets distorted, and what you imagine to be going on may actually not be happening at all. You are prone to flights of fancy, and at times your head is more than a little in the clouds.

It isn't natural for you to plan for the future, but it would be a good idea for you to do so. In the middle stage of your life, the phrase "easy come, easy go" definitely applies to you. No sooner has money come your way than it rapidly runs through your fingers like water. If you're not careful, you could be left without a penny.

**The Rounded Nose**

Yours is a nose for money and you can almost smell it. You make a good business partner, as you're reliable, stable and considerate. You'll make your money through hard (and honest) work, wise investments, and thrift. You can expect great satisfaction in your career during your forties.

Your forties will also be a good time for you personally. You can look forward to a happy and secure family life, where you will be surrounded by the love and support of those who are most important to you.

One of your most admirable qualities is that you're always ready to help a friend or loved one. If there's anything you can do to help make someone's life a little easier, you'll do it. And just knowing that you've helped is reward enough for you – you don't expect any kind of repayment.

**The Long Nose**

Your place is in the mainstream and you are a logical, straight thinker who could never be called irrational. You are a stable character, but at times this stability can develop in to pointless stubbornness.

You are an intelligent individual, and you use your brain power to plan for your future. Such plans are great, but you sometimes stick to them too rigidly. This means that if anything should go wrong, you could find yourself in an awkward position; you're not one of the most adaptable or innovative of people, and you can have difficulties coping with unexpected emergencies.

You have an amazing amount of self-control that you can learn to use to your benefit. But you expect others to have this quality too, and if anyone should fall short of your expectations, your intolerance shows.

For you, success is best achieved step by step. Use your intelligence to build firm financial foundations that will last into old age. Don't give in to deals that "guarantee" quick profits, as such things rarely pay off.

**The Short Nose**

It's really not surprising that you have many friends. Your sociable and easy-going nature means that you're enjoyable to be with and makes you a people magnet. You are a good friend, and you like to help others through their hard times, lending your optimism to worst-case scenarios, which helps to make things brighter somehow. You also give energetic encouragement, spurring people on to reach their goals; if only you could apply this to yourself.

You live very much in the here and now, and don't have many plans for the future – probably due to the fact that you aren't particularly ambitious.

Opportunities that others would jump at often come your way, but your lack of drive signifies that you usually don't act on them. All of this means that you won't have the most illustrious of careers, so it would be a good idea for you to devise some kind of saving strategy. You come into money sporadically, but it just doesn't seem to last long.

At the end of the day, though, you are one of those people who finds happiness no matter what happens.

**The Thin Nose**

This is considered to be the most attractive type of nose for both men and women. It gives the face an aloof appearance and aristocratic air. You are a perfectionist, and expect others to share your high standards. When they don't, you tend to be overly critical of them both personally and professionally.

You are a very strong person, and this sometimes develops into a domineering and manipulative attitude. This is great if you're a controlling officer in the military, but it's not particularly suited to the everyday workplace. Learn to control yourself before trying to control others if you want your career to reach its full potential. You are somewhat of a loner, and a more solitary profession or occupation would suit you best. Perhaps you should try writing (or at least something in the arts). Whatever you turn your hand to, your inner strength and perseverance means that success is probable.

You often choose to be alone instead of having to constantly compromise with someone (which you prefer *not* to do). This gives you a chance to concentrate on yourself and your own needs – which is what you enjoy most, and is also how you find your peace.

### The Curved (or Roman) Nose

Your strong will and ample amount of determination means that you are one of life's achievers. You are happy to take your time and make money slowly, gradually. You don't necessarily chase quick money and easy profits. You like to do things properly and thoroughly. Your intuition means that you quickly sense when something is amiss, and you steer clear of any kind of tricky dealings.

Your success can be found in the world of business. One of the things you enjoy most is clinching and closing a deal that others were chasing. You are very competitive by nature, but you also retain a sense of fair play. All of the above means that your chances of success are high – and you'll probably get all of its associated trappings, too!

You have a particular penchant for luxury and riches. Your ambition and drive combined with your business acumen means that you're likely to get what you want.


## THE FOUR UNUSUAL NOSES

### The Deer Nose
Like the thin nose, this has a flat bony bridge, but the tip is rounded. You are a friendly and warm-hearted individual. Problems may arise in your life often, but you manage to get through them without too many ill effects. Success will be yours, but not until the later stages of life.

### The Dragon Nose
This is a straight nose without any lumps or bumps. It's not too thin, but not too thick, and the tip is nicely rounded. This is the luckiest nose of all. Once you put your mind to it,

you can get anything and everything you want. You are a powerful but fair person, and you don't like to prey on those weaker than yourself.

### The Lion Nose
This is a strong, broad nose, again with a round tip. You can expect to make a good name for yourself and also earn the respect of others through hard work. You are likely to be wealthy in terms of finances and possessions. You are honest and kind, but will fight fiercely if necessary.

### The Sheep Nose
This is a particularly large nose with a bulbous tip and large but hidden nostrils. Success will be no stranger to you. In fact, you and Lady Luck are probably on first-name terms!! If you play your cards right and work hard and honestly, almost unlimited wealth could be yours.

## THE NOSTRILS
To complete your analysis of the nose, you mustn't forget to look at both the shape and size of your own or another person's nostrils.

**Round:** You are a great person to have as a friend. You're always ready to help a person out of a predicament with your innate ability to solve problems.

**Round and a Bit Flared:** This is the mark of a person who is good with their money and knows how to handle it.

**Oval:** This shape shows that you have an amazing amount of mental energy – your mind just never stops! You are a free spirit who doesn't like being in one place for too long.

**Square:** You have a huge amount of stamina and staying

power. You're not the kind of person who walks away from something or someone at the first sign of a problem.

**Triangular:** You will probably accumulate a good amount of wealth. You're not the sort of person who squanders money.

**Small and Thin:** Once you have money, you like to hold on to it! Be careful, though, otherwise you could become known as a miser.

**Small and Flat:** You may not make a large amount of money, so just make sure that you learn how to safeguard what you do have.

**Large and Flared:** You are very generous with your money and love to give to those you love.

**Large and Very Flared:** If you play your cards right and are sensible with your money, you could make yourself a very wealthy person.

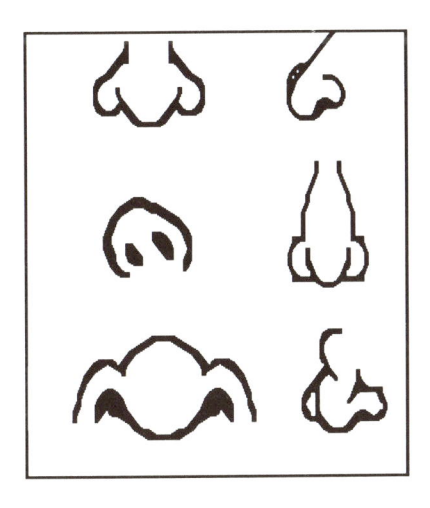

## THE PHILTRUM

The philtrum is the small groove that runs from your nose to the middle of your top lip. Some people say that humans have this feature to make it easier to drink from a bottle, but I'm sure there's no basis to that claim!

Examine your philtrum to find out info about y energy and vitality levels throughout your lifetime, and also to discover secrets about your sexual attitudes and to learn whether you will choose to have a large, medium or small family. There are four different types of philtrums.

### The Triangular Philtrum

The triangular philtrum is the ideal shape to have. It starts off being quite narrow at the nose, and then widens as it progresses down to your upper lip. This type is usually also deep and well defined. Such a shape shows that both mental and physical energies will last well into your old age. These energies are seen in your attitude and approach to life, and while your body may age, your mind will forever remain young and fresh. You can expect to remain sexually active throughout your lifetime, and you enjoy your sensuality within the secure walls of a loving relationship where you feel cherished and valued. You can expect to pour your energies into making your children's lives as enjoyable as possibly – and you're likely to have many children!

### The Parallel Philtrum

The parallel philtrum is of equal width from where it starts at your nose to where it reaches the middle of your top lip. Unless your parallel philtrum is also deep and very well defined, this type is not the most fortuitous. You may find that your energy levels are depleted throughout your lifetime by rocky romances and relationships. To avoid this, try and be careful when choosing partners; remember that you have an active role to play when beginning a new relationship, and don't let yourself be "chosen" all the time. Take your time and give yourself a chance to get to know a person properly before you dive feet first into a love-connection. Once you have found the right partner, it's likely that you will have one or two children rather than a huge family.

### The Inverted Triangular Philtrum

The inverted triangular philtrum is the opposite of the triangular philtrum, as it's wide at the base of your nose, narrowing down to your top lip. This type indicates that you will choose not to have a particularly large family, and if you do actually decide to become a parent, you'll only opt for one child. You have a moderate energy level that will remain stable throughout your lifetime. Although you enjoy intimacy with that special someone, you are not a sexually driven individual.

### The Flat Philtrum

This type of philtrum is not at all well defined. In fact, it may be so flat as to be invisible. You enjoy life to the full and look forward to having a family of your own. Your vitality will serve you well throughout the majority of your life, and as is perfectly natural, it will decline slightly in later years. You will go on to have an active and enjoyable retirement.

# THE PROFILE OF THE CHEEKBONES

**THE RIGHT CHEEKBONE**
TERRAIN – MOUNTAIN
MILESTONE OF LIFE – SECOND (31– 50 YEARS OF AGE)
MANSION – THE MANSION OF MARRIAGE (AFFAIRS)

**THE LEFT CHEEKBONE**
TERRAIN – MOUNTAIN
MILESTONE OF LIFE – SECOND (31-50 YEARS OF AGE)
MANSION – THE MANSION OF MARRIAGE (MARRIAGES / MARRIAGE-TYPE RELATIONSHIPS)

**THE CHEEKBONES**
Your cheekbones correspond to your attitude to life and the way in which you exercise your power and authority. You have to remember that these two things impact not only on your professional life, but on your home life, too. They will also affect your personal relationships. You must bear in mind that your cheekbones are mountains, and that you need to examine them in comparison to the other mountains (nose, forehead and chin) to decide on their prominence.

Moles in the upper section of your cheek (top half of your face), show that you have a very strong and determined mind. You need to make sure that you control this strength so that you don't become too domineering. Moles on the lower part of your cheeks are a good sign, but they point out that you are an inconsistent and emotional individual who may have difficulty sustaining a long-term relationship.

Although you will only see four categories of cheekbones in this section, there are actually five types; note that under the heading, "High Cheekbones," two slightly different types of cheekbones are considered.

**Strong Cheekbones**

The strength of your cheekbones represents your strength of character. Through hard work, you will reach a high-status position. You're not only determined, but also very charming. The domineering aspects of your personality, however, sometimes overshadow this charm.

You are best suited to a position of authority where it's your job to oversee others and be in control. There is something about you which makes people sit up, take notice and listen. You'll do well in a high-pressure job where you are able to flex your metaphorical muscles and get your teeth into your work. Your chances of a successful career are great. It's a different story in your personal life, though.

You find it very difficult to delegate even the smallest amount of responsibility to another person. You're just not one of life's compromising sharers. Unless you find and expose your softer side, and learn how to lay down your weapons in the name of love, you would be wise to live alone. This is a drastic option, though, and there's no reason why you can't use your determination and will power to control the negative aspects of your character to find love, companionship and happiness.

**High Cheekbones**

These show that you have the ability to reach a high

occupational level. High, square cheekbones show that you have the strength of character needed to command, while also possessing a sense of fair play. You're not drunk with power, and have a good mental balance, as well as an admirable way of dealing with people.

This is not quite the case with high, rounded cheekbones. This means that you have the need to dominate other people and situations. You usually try to do this through your work, but you still don't get the respect and recognition that you yearn for so much. You won't reach the top of your profession, since your superiors don't give you the power that you desire. Either you make do with a moderate level of success, or you rebel.

Whether rounded or square, neither type of high cheekbones bodes particularly well for a satisfactory home life. You're a very difficult person to live with, in that you find it hard to compromise; you like everything to be done *your* way. The truth is this: if you can find a way to let go a little, you will be a lot less angry, and far happier in yourself *and* your most precious relationship.

**Cheekbones that are Near to the Nose**

The nearer your cheekbones are to your nose, the more difficult you are to get along with. If you're not careful, you'll lose your friends through your selfishness. Your unwillingness to compromise could mean that you're holding yourself back in your career. You must be able to adapt and to give as well as take to make it in the business world – even at the highest levels. You can be cruel, so you really need to watch your behavior and moderate it accordingly.

If these narrow cheekbones aren't really near to your

nose and a little width remains, you may be a fortunate person; you'll probably find that things just fall in to your lap, and that promotions come to you without you having to chase them or work too hard. This is not to say, however, that you can afford to become complacent about your professional position.

**Flat Cheekbones**

You're easy to get along with and you're also pretty laid-back and relaxed; you're not a difficult person at all! You'll probably end up being your own boss one day, as you don't really appreciate having to answer to someone. You're unlikely to experience a phenomenal amount of success since you're not the most ambitious of people, and you don't really push yourself. Besides, a high-powered position doesn't appeal to you that much anyway – you can't be bothered to deal with all the stress that comes with such a job.

You are likely to have a happy and relatively peaceful home life without many upheavals or arguments – creating or perpetuating stress and strife is simply not your style.

# THE PROFILE OF THE MOUTH

TERRAIN – RIVER
VITAL ENERGY – FLEXIBILITY
FATE – WEALTH
PLANET – MERCURY
MILESTONE OF LIFE – THIRD (50 YEARS OF AGE AND ONWARDS)
FACIAL MANSION – THE MANSIONS OF THE HOME

### THE MOUTH

By examining your mouth, you can glean information about your personality and also your attitude to others. The mouth has always been linked to sexuality – especially in women. Since tribal times, the lips have been painted or dyed in an attempt to enhance their appearance, and also to help attract a mate. This practice still goes on today (and is far more widespread now); just look at the massive profits made today by the cosmetics industry in the sales of lipstick.

When considering your own or someone else's mouth, you need to look at the size of the mouth (in relation to the other facial features), the shape, the color and also how the mouth is held.

Ideally, your mouth should be moist, with a nice pink color – neither too dark nor too pale. The bottom and top lips should be of equal width and fullness, with a defined outline and neatly meeting corners. The lips should be firm but not hard, tight or tense. Thin and tight lips show a person to be stubborn or emotionally hard. A thin upper lip indicates that an individual is competitive and sometime argumentative. A short upper lip means that a person may have problems in later life that are caused by a lack of self-control.

A mole on a person's upper lip shows that this individual enjoys being pampered and indulged, but also enjoys showering the finer things in life upon his or her loved ones! This person also has high standard in every area of life; the problem is that everyone else is also expected to have such standards.

There are a total of ten different types of mouth. You'll see that seven of these are the more common categories, while the other three are the more unusual types of mouth.

## THE SEVEN BASIC MOUTH TYPES

### The Full and Well-Balanced Mouth

Your top and bottom lips are of equal size and the corners meet nicely. These lips look near perfect and they are almost symmetrical. You have a balanced and well-rounded personality and an even temper. You enjoy being with people; you're friendly, caring and openly expressive. Reliability is your middle name, and you're not one to run from responsibility. You are only too happy to lighten a friend's load and help in any way you can – and you're often very helpful since you're such a good problem-solver.

You have an amazing ability to keep cool, even when those around you are running around like headless chickens! You seem to exude calmness and control. For these reasons, you are good at dealing with both small and large groups of people. You use your ability to adapt to almost any situation and to soothe agitated people, or just to help make others feel more relaxed and at ease. You will move (or mold) heaven and earth to make sure that your own life, as well as the lives of those you love, runs as easily and as freely from stress as possible.

You are dependable but not boring. There's nothing you enjoy more than having a laugh and fooling around with your friends at a spontaneous get-together.

You make a good parent, mixing fun and joviality with care and authority.

### The Thin, Long Mouth

Well, aren't you a strong-willed individual with plenty of courage and gumption! You are also more than a little stubborn; once you've made your mind up to do or get something (whether for the right or wrong reasons), there is precious little anyone can do to make you alter your course of action.

You're not born to follow someone else's instructions blindly. Instead, you prefer to lead and control other people and situations. But you can be overly domineering at times. If all of this sounds a little negative, don't be alarmed – you have good qualities, too!

When someone has earned your trust and respect, you become a very loyal friend, one who is always there to give support. Your caring and compassionate side just won't let you turn your back on a person in need. You can't stand to see anyone being mistreated or picked on for no good reason. Your sense of fair play won't stand for it. If only you could learn to control your domineering aspects, you would have less of a name for being a tyrant. You'll probably loosen up of your own accord as you get older. Also, you might want to try talking less and listening more to what others are thinking and feeling.

As a parent you are very much the disciplinarian, but you will raise happy and well-adjusted children.

### The Small Mouth

Your mouth may be small, but your mind is very big! Sometimes, though, your mind is too open. Imagination is a wonderful thing so long as it's kept within limits; you tend to become fanciful, even fantastical. Try and keep one foot on the ground – for your own good. Your inclination toward dreaming, or distorting the truth, is symbolic of your overindulgent nature.

You can be sociable once you put your mind to it, but this is through necessity rather than choice. You prefer to be alone, and maybe this is not such a bad thing, since you can be self-centered and highly intolerant of others. This intolerance belies truths about how you feel about yourself. You are a perfectionist and you're very hard on yourself if you fail to reach the high standards you set for yourself. If others don't meet these standards, your wrath shows. Your inner strength means that you're constantly striving to improve yourself. Just learn not to push yourself too hard.

As you get older, it's likely that you'll become more sociable and easy-going. It's then that people will discover how intelligent and insightful you really are. If only you used your determination to show these qualities at an early stage of your life, things could be very different.

**The Turned-Up Mouth**

You always look like you're about to break in to a huge dazzling smile! You're a cheerful person with a brilliant sense of humor. You've got a naturally happy disposition, and all this combines to make you a regular ray of sunshine. You're a very active person who finds it hard to just sit still and do nothing – you'd much rather be out with your friends. This active and energetic nature, however, can manifest itself in a kind of restlessness, which means that you're probably always flitting from one thing to the next.

You're very considerate of others and are a really friendly person. You like to see others enjoying themselves, and you make sure that your guests are happy, relaxed, and made to feel welcome in your circle.

When you have problems, you don't dwell on them. Indeed, you laugh in the face of adversity – and you expect others to do the same. You have neither the time nor the inclination to help those who refuse to help themselves. You simply can't stand people who wallow in misfortune. If there's a problem, do something about it – don't just cry over split milk!

Your casual approach to life is all very well, but you can't afford to be too laid-back. You have little enough regard for the present, and you make practically no provision for your future. You will start to take things more seriously as you grow older.

Your children will love you. Becoming a parent will be a good excuse for you to return to your childhood, and you'll enjoy playing around and having childish fun – and your little ones will have a ball too!

**The Turned-Down Mouth**
This mouth may make you look as though you're feeling a little bit sad, or as if you have the weight of the world on your shoulders, even when you're totally happy inside. This type of mouth points to negative personality traits. You are a domineering and difficult person. When you want something, you won't be happy until you get it – at any cost. The truth is, though, that even when your demands are met, you still want more. You're never satisfied, and for this reason you could be called greedy. You are far better at taking than you are at giving, although you would never acknowledge this fact. If you could control these negative aspects of your character, you could do very well in life (and you'd be a lot happier, too).

You are extremely strong-willed (some would say stubborn!), and when you have your sights on something, nothing can get in your way. You can be very hard on people, and if someone crosses you even once, you expel them from your life; but then you sometimes become depressed because you feel alienated or abandoned. Although you have unrealistic expectations of others, you are more than happy to let them run around after you. Just try to make sure that you don't let yourself become lazy or even slovenly!

You must learn to be more considerate of others, and you need to stop taking life so seriously. You would be so much better off if you didn't treat each of your problems like it was the end of the world – you can contend and cope with far more than you realize!

**The Bow-Shaped Mouth**

You are difficult to please and you never really let anyone in (not easily anyway). This means that you quickly earn yourself the reputation of being a superficial and shallow person.

You're sociable, but only up to a point. While you like being around people, you insist on keeping them at arm's length (using arrogance to do so). Not all of this is exactly your fault; you simply find it hard to trust people and to believe in friendship. Perhaps you need to build up your self-confidence; you have to believe in yourself to understand how others could like you and choose to be in your company.

Once you have overcome your suspicions, insecurities and cynicism, you have the ability to become a very different person. When you have achieved closeness with someone, you'll find that you actually do have a lot to offer, and that in fact you enjoy sharing a special warmth and bond. You should find that as you get older, it becomes easier to forge friendships and rewarding relationships.

### Cupid's Bow Mouth

This is the mouth of a very loving person. If your aura could be seen, it would be made up of all the warmest colors. You don't often lose your temper – you're far too calm and peaceful for that – and you seem to have almost endless amounts of tolerance and understanding. These qualities are the same in both men and women with this type of mouth.

Women with this mouth are extremely loving, and usually enjoy successful marriages; they are also more likely to get married at a relatively young age than those who don't have this mouth. While you may work in paid employment outside of your home, you are also very active on the domestic front. Your husband and children will be surrounded by warmth and affection, comfortable in the knowledge that they have your love.

In contrast, if you are a male, you will probably marry later in life. It's not that you enjoy being free to have many sexual partners – it's just that you enjoy living alone in a home that is exactly the way you want it to be. You are a very warm person, but you enjoy having your own private space and place to live in. You'll find that you have many female friends because you're very aware of your feminine energies, and you have a deep understanding of the female psyche and sexuality. Sympathy, empathy, and respect are what get you female attention. For this, other men may envy you. But you don't use this attention to gain sexual favors; you treat each woman as a friend, with respect and esteem.

Whatever sex you are, male or female, you will have many friends in your life, as you see people for who, not what, they are.

## THE THREE UNUSUAL MOUTHS

### The Ox Mouth
This is a big mouth, with both lips equal in size. It is characterized by the lips having a straight outline. You will make many friends throughout the course of your colorful life. You're easy to like because of your warmth and openly displayed affection. You value and know how to maintain a deep and strong bond of friendship. People often come to you in times of trouble or need, when they're seeking some sort of calmness and tranquillity in a strong, serene sanctuary.

### The Dragon Mouth
This is a generous mouth, with a clearly defined outline, distinctly sharp corners and a beautiful, rich color. This mouth stands out simply because it looks almost perfect. It often looks made-up, even if you are not wearing lipstick. You are an extremely fortunate person. Even though your life may be hard, you continue to fight. You emerge from black times as a kind, balanced, and strong individual. You use every experience you have, good or bad, to develop a clear perspective and a broad view of life. With such determination, strength, and resilience, this mouth shows the world that you are a force to be reckoned with.

### The Tiger Mouth
This is an extremely big mouth that is covered with generous, full lips. The mouth is usually held closed, but not tightly clamped shut. It signifies that you are a good person, who is kind and fair. Having said that, you are certainly *not* a person to offend, insult, or cross. You will do well, receiving

the respect of others and reaching high levels of success in whatever you choose to make the focus of your life.

## THE SIGNIFICANCE OF LINES ROUND YOUR MOUTH

To ensure that you have made an accurate and detailed analysis of the mouth, remember that you must also take notice of the lines in this area. These lines are like tiny rays of light, each giving a new piece of information about personality and character.

Purse your lips and you'll notice that small vertical grooves appear along your top lip. In later life, these grooves may become permanent lines. People who have these lines have probably spent a good deal of their life pinching their lips together in self-righteous judgmental poses, temper, or just plain sulking. It's a sign of a somewhat selfish person who is only happy so long as they're getting their own way. Such people can be very difficult and even cold characters, who are demanding and hard to please – you have been warned!

### Laugh Lines

Laugh lines run from the nose diagonally down toward the mouth and then out toward the chin. We only usually see these lines when a person smiles or laughs (hence their name), or in people in mid-life. If these lines can easily be seen in the relaxed face of a younger person, it is not a particularly good sign. From around the age of forty and onward, though, these lines are a fortunate symbol. The length and span of the lines tell us about your energy levels throughout your life-time.

### Gently Curved Lines of Average Length
You can expect to live out your normal life span happily – as long as you look after yourself properly, that is! To have lines of this shape and type denotes a good life (despite troubles), and a happy retirement. You are very fortunate.

### Long Lines that Curve Outwards
These are the best kind of laugh lines to have. A very high amount of energy is depicted – one which should last throughout your lifetime. It's likely that if you look after yourself and your health properly, you will live to see several generations of successors – and that's a long time! Make sure that you remain physically fit and mentally active as you grow older.

### Long Lines that Curve in Below the Mouth
The long length of these lines echoes the long length of life seen in the analysis above. So long as you hold on to your *joie de vivre* and conquer the negative aspects of your personality, you will have a comfortable old age. But if you insist on being difficult, you could just end up with very few people in your life. Ultimately, who you end your life with is up to you and your behavior.

### Short Lines that Curve in to the Corners of the Mouth
These lines support an average length of life with a good supply of energy. You need to make provision for your future financial security as early as you can. While guarding against future poverty and hardships, you'll also be preparing yourself for when you retire – and what a retirement you'll have!

## THE TEETH

It is also worth examining teeth when performing a face reading. Ideally, everyone should have all thirty-two teeth. In reality, though, very few of us make it to adulthood with all of our teeth. Nearly all of us have problems with our wisdom teeth (usually before they are removed!), and many people also have teeth removed to have braces fitted during their teenage years. For those of you who *do* have every tooth –

then be happy! You are a very blessed individual, with luck and good fortune on your side! If your teeth are also straight, a nice bright color, and they fit snugly together, you are destined for a life of optimal well-being and happiness. Even though you may have bad times – we all do – for you, these will be greatly outweighed by good times. Teeth with rounded edges also portend a good future.

If you have smaller teeth and very exposed and noticeable gums, you tend to be a little selfish, and sometimes you only concentrate on your own needs, oblivious to the needs of others. Try to be a little more giving, and you'll find that your life will change for the better.

Perhaps your teeth are the opposite and they are in fact quite large or long. This represents longevity and also that the long path of your life will not be free from troubles and strife. But don't fear! You are intelligent, resilient, and ambitious enough to survive pretty much whatever life throws at you. And you can bet your bottom dollar that in the long run you'll only benefit in some way from any negativity that enters your life.

The two front teeth have a slightly different significance. The left tooth is associated to your sense of patriotism. The right relates directly to your family. If either of these is crooked, it indicates a weaker link, tie or even feeling of duty than would normally be seen or expected.

Finally, teeth that don't sit straight, but instead slope or slant inwards show that your strength of character is such that you don't fear being alone. Indeed, it may even be the case that your batteries are only ever truly recharged if you do get to spend time alone.

# THE PROFILE OF THE CHIN

TERRAIN – MOUNTAIN
MILESTONE OF LIFE – THIRD (50 YEARS OF AGE AND ONWARDS)
FACIAL MANSIONS – NONE

### THE CHIN

Your chin gives away secrets about your inner strength. By looking at a person's chin, you can learn if they are overly stubborn – or even aggressive – or if a person is lacking in self-confidence and belief in himself. Levels of inner strength can affect every part of your life – from how you perform in professional and work-related situations to how you acquit yourself in your personal affairs. Don't underestimate the significance of your own or someone else's chin, and be sure to refer to the other facial features too.

The ideal chin is squarish with rounded corners – not sharp angles. This kind of chin is a good sign for all aspects of a person's life. It shows a good level of energy and a perseverance that will last a lifetime.

A mole on or towards the edge of your chin shows that you are a person who is essentially a romantic who adores getting two people together in a love-connection. What you need to understand is that it's not always acceptable (or wise) to interfere in other people's business – even if your intentions are good!

There are seven different types of chin. Pay particular attention to the "Pointed Chin," where you'll see that a very subtle difference in structure can make a huge difference in personality. You also need to make sure that you don't get the "Pointed Chin" confused with the "Protruding Chin."

## THE SEVEN CHIN TYPES

### The Round Chin
You do have inner strength, but you tend to keep it well hidden, and you're prone to letting other people impose their will on you. You're a likable person, but apathy like this will not help you to find happiness. Learn to flex your mental muscle and make sure that you make your own way in life. Be true to yourself, be strong and everything else will follow.

### The Oval Chin
You will use your inner strength in the first and second stages of your life to make your old age secure. You'll find that when you reach your sunset years, your energy and strength will diminish (as is natural), but by that time you'll have everything you need, and you won't have to worry. One last thing, though – you must learn to control your impulsive behavior and develop an understanding of the importance of having good sense.

### The Square Chin
Nobody could call you a weak individual! In fact, you have a little too much inner strength, and you're prone to obstinacy. When you want something, even if there's no real reason for you to have it, you set your chin, grit your teeth, dig your heels in, and nothing or no one can change your

mind or budge you from your course. Believing in yourself and being strong-willed are not bad qualities, but stubbornness is not an attractive thing when taken to the extreme.

**The Pointy Chin**
Just as your pointy chin is narrow, so is your mind. Your weakness lies in your inability to make a decision and then to stick to it. What you believe today isn't necessarily what you'll believe tomorrow. You need to try and stick to your guns and stop being so gullible. You can be easily fooled or led astray by people who are not really worthy of you or your friendship. These traits point to a lack of self-esteem; try to develop more self-confidence.

**The Protruding Chin**
You really need to control your inner strength, otherwise you could find yourself alone. There is a time and a place for controlled aggression (have you ever tried sports?), but you don't seem to understand this. Indeed, you appear to thrive on animosity and hostility. You need to realize that such emotions will only bring discord, disharmony and dissatisfaction to your life.

**The Receding Chin**
This is a very small and weak-looking chin, which signifies a small amount of inner strength. Without such strength and energy, it is unlikely that you will ever reach your goal. You could do very well in life if you develop determination, perseverance and confidence. What's the point in having dreams if you're not going to work towards making any of them come true?

### The Cleft Chin
This chin is characterized by either a little or large dip or groove in the middle of it. You have strength in terms of your adventurous spirit, and you like to make huge leaps of faith without worrying about future consequences. This is admirable only when kept within certain limits; beyond sensible boundaries, it looks foolish. Make sure that you don't develop a reckless lack of regard. You don't plan for the future because you don't like to be committed to anything; you have to be free to take off in a different direction should the mood take you.

The more pronounced the cleft, the more pronounced the characteristics. You would benefit from maturing without losing your love of freedom and valuable independence.


### THE JAW-LINE
Everybody wants to be successful in his or her chosen career. We all want to be the best that we can be, and we all want to be accorded the respect of our colleagues and peers. Your jaw-line is directly related to the subject of success and status. The shape of your jaw-line contains information about your attitude toward achieving success and status, and by examining this part of your face, you can get some ideas on how you should go about reaching your goals.

Ideally, the jaw-line is well-defined and has a solid strong shape. The jaw-line should be neither wider nor narrower than the forehead. The ideal jaw-line is also softly curved rather than having sharply squared corners. The ideally shaped jaw-line shows someone who is knowledgeable, intelligent and well adjusted. The owner of this type of jaw-line is destined for success and can expect a healthy and progressive career. It is also likely that he or she will reach a high position of power while still managing to hold a respectable office. This jaw-line belongs to a fair individual who won't let power and status go to his or her head, and who refuses to tolerate injustices, harassment or underhand dealings in or out of the workplace. If this jaw-line belongs to you, it signifies that you are a strong person. You have a fist of iron and when your gloves come off, you are most certainly a force to be reckoned with. You will work well and make a good name for yourself, and you will also be well respected by the powers that be.

When examining your jaw-line, make sure that you keep it separate from your chin. The chin has its own distinctive significance and it should not be confused with your jaw. Aside from the above-mentioned "ideal" jaw-line, there are a further five types.

**The Narrow Jaw-Line**

If your jaw-line is not particularly wide but is actually narrow, than you need to have an extra amount of energy and determination. Your narrow jaw-line denotes that a lack of perseverance and long-lasting drive may hinder you when trying to reach your goals. While you do have a pathway to success, achievement, and all the associated prestige and status stretching out in front of you, you must be certain that you have the energy reserves needed to reach the road's end.

You *can* get everything that you desire – just as long as you learn not to give up at the first hurdle.

**The Tapering Jaw-Line**

This type is different than the narrow jaw-line in that the tapering jaw-line is wide at its base, and then narrows markedly as it slopes in to the chin. You will usually find this type of jaw-line as the lower section of an oval face.

It is likely to be the case that success and status will both be yours without you having to expend too much effort or hard work. Make sure that you don't take such success for granted – and remember that it might not last forever. Provided that you are prudent and that you use your success wisely, you will be free to go forth and enjoy the later stages of your life. You will probably achieve your goals in life, but be certain to plan properly for your old age so that when the time comes for you to retire, you can do so with complete confidence.

**The Round Jaw-Line**

You are a very fortunate individual! It's likely that your childhood and family history are full of happy memories, stability and love. It's highly probable that your parents instilled into you a strong work ethic, and also an ambition for achievement, success and status.

You may have been born into a family that was comfortably well-off (though not necessarily rich), and you will manage to maintain this level of comfort without wanting to climb too high up the ladder of success. You are ambitious, but you don't strive to reach the top echelons of the business world. You will make a good name for yourself and will enjoy respect and a moderate level of status.

**The Square Jaw-Line**
You will work hard to obtain the level of success and status that you desire. You will utilize your skills, strengths, and stubborn streak to propel you toward your goals. The square jaw-line reflects the stability of your character – another quality that will aid you on your journey to the top. A word of warning, though: while your focused energies and stubbornness will help to propel you toward promotion and progress, you must make sure that these things don't damage your personal life. Selfishness and an inability to compromise may only prove to alienate those you care about the most. And what good is success and status if you have no one to share them with?

**The Broad Jaw-Line with Prominent Corners**
There is really no doubt that you will attain a high level of success and status, you can be sure that through hard work and effort you will secure yourself a good position and do well. You certainly have the energy, skills, and drive to get to the top. How you behave when you get there, however, is quite another matter.

Your wide jaw-line looks strong and powerful – qualities

that are present in your character in abundance. Sometimes, however, your personality can be a little too controlling, and if someone chooses not to do your bidding, you will back them into a corner and keep them there until they cave in and submit to your will. This desire to dominate is all very good and well if you're in the military, but it does not sit well in everyday civilian life. You must learn the skills and value of teamwork, diplomacy and compromise. You need to realize that the respect of others must be earned and that it is not simply given for free. To earn such respect, you need to develop understanding and compassion, and to become less controlling, forceful and hard. After all, success, status and power could all be yours, but what do these three things mean if you don't have good people skills and the respect of those with whom you work?